As We Are

Don Clark, Ph.D.

AS WE ARE

Alyson Publications • Boston

Other books by Don Clark

Loving Someone Gay

Living Gay

The New Loving Someone Gay

Published as a trade paperback original by
Alyson Publications,
40 Plympton Street,
Boston, Mass. 02118.

Distributed in the U.K. by GMP Publishers,
PO Box 247, London, N15 6RW, England.

First U.S. edition: April, 1988

Library of Congress Cataloging-in-Publication Data

Clark, Donald H., 1930-
"As we are."

1. Gays — United States. 2. Gay men — United States.
3. AIDS (Disease) — Social aspects — United States.
I. Title.
HQ76.3.U5C58 1988 306.7′662 87-72880
ISBN 1-55583-127-3 (pbk.)

Contents

For the good
who have gone early
and are well
remembered.

Preface

The gay community is in crisis and a new sense of our identity is emerging. The process of self-discovery, already under way, has been accelerated by the stunning impact that the AIDS epidemic has had on our community.

We have found inner resources that we had only glimpsed before. We have learned that our lives truly depend upon throwing off the identity given to us by the surrounding world and making our own difficult discovery of ourselves, individually and collectively.

We are now engaged in an agonizing, yet richly rewarding, process of change. We are finding our real goodness and strength as we love and care for one another. We are discovering our spirituality and our unique ability to cooperate with change. The discoveries we have made in one decade would be cause for great pride in any community.

Part One

LOVING

Happiness

By ironic chance we are known today as *gay* people. We have had other names in the past and will have other names in the future. Yet, as the word's alternate meaning implies, we are happy people. That does not mean life is easy or tranquil for us, but most of us learn more about happiness in our lifetimes than we are able to communicate.

Happiness is the great paradox of human experience. Search for it and it will elude you. Turn your back, busy yourself with your life's task, and happiness will envelop you. And the paradox of happiness contains the equally mysterious paradox of love. Happiness born of love is the most enchanting variety. Give more love than you receive; only then will you receive more love than you give.

When I was a very young psychologist in New York City, teaching, doing research, and trying to learn the art of the clinician, I met a wonderful older woman who had been trained as an orthodox psychoanalyst. Orthodox psychoanalysis already represented the old guard and I was prepared to view her with all the suspicion that can be mustered by a rebel with unclear causes.

But she was disarming. I could feel that she liked me. And I liked her. She was devoted to common sense and human welfare, and for her these values came before any dogma.

I was interested in learning as much as I could about the new, evolving forms of group psychotherapy. She was interested in the application of group psychotherapy techniques in work with young children. It was a match. I was willing to go into the fish-bowl with the children, as the experimenting neophyte therapist watched by other would-be learners through one-way vision mirrors, and she was willing to be my mentor as we explored the terrain together.

It led to a wonderful, loving friendship in which we were able to transcend the stuffy form of a professional relationship and learn more by confessing our doubts and wonder to one another.

We were sitting at her sunny breakfast table on Park Avenue very early one morning, the tape recorder running as we fumbled with the concepts of a book we were beginning to write together. My friend had been born in Russia, had lived and trained in Europe, and had seen enough of the world to make me take her words seriously.

That morning I asked her, "How is a person to go about achieving happiness?"

Her response was so sudden and intense it startled me. "That's no good," she said. "You don't achieve happiness. You go chasing it and you waste your life. You must look for *satisfaction*. Find out who you are. Be that. Make your life satisfying. Then comes happiness — free."

It seemed to be a part of our discussion of the moment and not meant as advice for me. But I have never forgotten it. When the time was ripe for me to claim my gay identity, to "come out" both in my professional and personal worlds, I worried about telling her. I need not have worried. Her sane humanitarian values were what made her the wonderful person she was, not her training in this institute or that. She listened, raised her eyebrows, and said simply, "I trust you."

Later, I began leading gay weekend groups in New York

City. I did not hide what I was doing, but I did not advertise it either. I knew it was right and helpful, but I was still intimidated by the psychiatry, psychology, and social work establishments that were inclined to be less than kind to anyone stepping out of line. And being a publicly gay psychologist was still considered way out of line — gayness was classified as a mental illness, in fact.

My friend heard all the rumors that swept through the psychoanalytic canyons of New York City, since many of the analysts were her patients. One evening, my wife and I were at her apartment, about to go out to dinner. As my friend pinned her hat into place, she mentioned a distorted story that she had heard. She correctly suspected it was the product of homophobia and salacious imagination. "Somebody told me you are having groups for homosexual men and that you are having them sit around in a circle and masturbate. I said I didn't believe it, but if you *were* doing such a thing it must be for some very good reason." Period. End of conversation. She did not need to hear my disclaimer.

The euphemism of "lovemaking" that is used to describe sexual activity in polite terms masks the still-existing belief that sexual intercourse is neither polite nor nice. The confusion around words continues to cause trouble. In those first gay groups I found that gay people were understandably wary, living as they did in a judgmental environment, but they had a great need to bring love to one another. They did not come to a weekend group to indulge in sexual activity — that was readily available in New York City.

But I must thank our detractors, especially the rumor mongers. Their repeated sly suggestions that sex was the purpose of gay therapy and support groups sensitized me to the obvious in our collective gay nature. Our homophobic critics envy us, imagining us as indulgent creatures who live from one orgasm to the next. At times they have even been successful in convincing many of us that this is true.

The truth is that our sexuality was so threatened, and thus hidden, for so many years that when our turn at liberation came along, at first many of us saw liberation simply as the freedom to have sex more frequently. But, for most, orgiastic celebration did not last long. Gay people continued to recognize the value of sex, but soon we began to ask what else there was. We had begun to pick ourselves up and look for the rest of our identity long before sexually transmitted disease became a threat to our lives.

What the general population was noticing about us subliminally was how much we seem to need to move toward one another with arms open and affection showing. It is remarkable to see such vulnerability in a world that worries so much about security and spends so much money on locks and guns.

We gays deserve neither blame nor credit for it, since it is no more and no less than a part of our nature. Nor do we restrict our expression of love to interaction with other gay people. Certainly it is not restricted to potential sexual partners. We thrive on the facilitation of love anywhere and with every imaginable kind of people.

One gay man told me a story I have heard in many variations. He was with the U.S. military in Vietnam. Like many, he referred to those years as his "mistake" in life. Late one afternoon he was separated from his patrol and wondered if he should try to find a safe place to hide until morning. "I was crawling toward this bush, and then I saw another guy about twenty yards away, alone and crawling toward another bush. Skin color and uniform identified us as enemies. We sort of pretended not to see each other. I could tell he was scared too. He looked like a kid. After a very long half-hour behind our bushes we looked each other in the eye. It certainly wasn't the same as cruising but it did give me that funny feeling you get when you cruise some guy. He still looked as scared as I was. We both had weapons and I'm sure we were both conscious of it. But I couldn't use that weapon and neither could he. It was absurd. We sneaked looks at each other for what seemed a very long time. Then a weird thing happened. He smiled. I bet he was about sixteen years old. Scared as I was, I smiled too — maybe because I was scared. Then he waved at me and moved off in a different direction. I suppose if I'd told my patrol leader what happened he'd have shot me. Hell, if it was a different time and place, we might have ended up bed partners, or at least friends."

And a young lesbian told me of striking up a conversation with an even younger male hustler on an urban street corner. "Honey", she said, "he told me he was straight and I believed it. He also told me why he couldn't go home again and I believed that too. So I packed him off in my car to meet a nice gay man I know who is a fatherly type. He found the kid a home and saw to it that the parents were told the boy was okay. The kid's now pulling down B-pluses in school. So if you hear about me out cruising the streets...," she laughed.

How do we come by happiness? It is that elusive feeling of well-being that cannot be grasped directly. One cannot buy happiness, earn it, or inherit it. But you can be helped to learn about it. For many, that help comes from gay people.

Happiness is most likely to find you when you are fully present in the moment. It is very easy to enter the future or the past in thoughts and emotions. This can produce nostalgia and hope, the memories of happiness past and the wish for happiness to come. But happiness itself can be experienced only in the present moment. That is what makes it so precious to us.

To experience it in the present, you must be balanced. It is fair to say that happiness *is* the experience of balance. The various forces inside you must be balanced and you must be in balance in relation to the world around you. Happiness is almost invariably accompanied by a willingness to give and accept love. Sometimes we are wanting but not willing. Defenses must be down and the willingness must be there. Love is not something you shop for; rather it is something you yield to. Being unwilling to accept or give love makes you inhospitable to happiness.

Someone once described this to me so vividly that I wrote it down: "I realized that happiness was *possible* when I became aware of my feelings of love — my love for his body, his intelligence, his emotions, his heart, and his spirit. But happiness began to live and breathe when I became aware of his feelings of love for me —

his love of my body, my intellect, my emotions, my heart and my spirit."

Happiness is balance, balance of the many forces within you, and balance of the self amid the many forces outside you. We speak of the happy-go-lucky person who is constantly in pursuit of pleasure and leads a perfectly unexamined life as if that person were happy. That person is a myth. Humans are reflective creatures. We have awareness of the self and we have little choice about being confronted with the consequences of our behavior.

Sages throughout history have warned that, if you hope to find peace and permit happiness to find you, it is necessary to examine yourself so you can move beyond the small preoccupation with self. That is easier said than done. It requires courage and honesty. Psychotherapy can help if both you and the psychotherapist are honest and care for one another. Moments in nature can be equally meaningful, granting perspective while you are immersed in the transcendent beauty of trees, ocean, mountains or desert. You learn about yourself most easily when there is no need to hide.

Unfortunately, we are taught while youngsters to present a facade to the world. We are told what is desirable, and we try to arrange the externals of self to present the appropriate picture. It is a lie, of course, and we pay the price for hiding the true self: love and acceptance from others is directed to the facade that we present. We do not receive the feelings deeply because they are aimed at the surface.

It is true that some social control of behavior is required if people are to live together amiably. But behavior can be controlled in a healthy way when we can afford to be absolutely honest in communicating our feelings. It is not our feelings that are destructive or anti-social, it is our behavior. Because we try to hide and distort our feelings, we create additional feelings, ugly in mutation and dangerous if our controls slip and these mutated feelings become the basis of behavior. It is possible to accept one another's simple basic feelings honestly and meet one another's true needs but we seldom do. We are too protective of our real and imagined greed and power.

Gay people seem to have a hard life. We are hurt often, not only by sticks and stones, but also by the names we are called. We, who need so strongly to love, are seen as frighteningly different. People feel they must socially isolate us. It is true that we pose a loving threat to contemporary adversarial societies. Our "threat" contains the solution to ever-escalating hostility, but fearful people are made even more fearful when confronted with human difference. And we are different.

The difficult life most gay people must live, particularly in their early years, makes us ready to examine the self, however. We start, long before most people, to wonder who we are. Told that we are bad, we are not as frightened to search for our faults and try to correct them. And yet, this strange beginning makes us most suspicious of our discovered virtues.

One way or another, we continue throughout our lifetimes to learn more about who we are. And the more we know, the better we are able to find our balance. As we grow older, we are more likely to embrace acceptance and to be captured by happiness.

How terribly discouraging it is to open a large unabridged dictionary and find the first definition for love listed as "the profoundly tender or passionate affection for a person of the opposite sex." I wonder how those who agreed on that definition came to it. I wonder if it is the only way they have known to achieve balance.

Many societies try as hard as they can to divide human characteristics, emotions, attitudes, and tasks into those considered appropriate for women and those which are appropriate for men. This places a terrific strain on every individual, since we all have some of the emotions, attitudes and aptitudes prescribed for "the other sex"; it also reflects the common cultural prejudice that there is superior utility in heterosexuality. Presumably, if you want to find the way to the rest of yourself, it can only be done in the company of someone of a different gender. This sort of prejudice makes it very difficult to get to know yourself in a truthful way.

It makes sense to me that the reason educated people in Western society have become so enamoured with psychotherapy in this century is that it offers some hope of burrowing beneath societal prohibitions and finding out who you truly are. I also believe I understand why such a large number of people are waking up suddenly and demanding we try to protect the environment where it has not already been mutilated. These people sense that nature is a place where they can learn about themselves when they are ready.

I remember a man whom the world considered very important coming into my office a few years ago because he felt, in his own words, "off balance." He had learned that he could not get rid of his homosexual feelings, though he had posed as one of the born-again success stories of a psychotherapist who claims to "cure" gay people of being themselves. But his persistent homosexual feelings interfered with his very important job and his socially appropriate marriage. During the entire visit, he never sat down. He paced in front of my chair so that I was forced to look up at him. He shook his finger at me. "I know I have to learn more about myself but I have no intention of digging around in all that muck and mire you people wallow in. I just want to get things in order."

It was not possible for us to work together. He was not ready or willing to know himself. He was frightened because he was aware that he was out of balance, but there was no way for him to become balanced because he was unwilling to face the parts of himself that were still waiting to be admitted to consciousness.

People who are not gay and who do not suffer from homophobia, bigotry, or the widespread problem of prejudice often comment that so many of their gay friends seem more broadminded, tolerant and fair, or can more easily see both sides of an argument. That makes a lot of sense. It is easy to forget that the ability of a man to fully love another man or a woman to fully love another woman is a gift. We gays are not stuck with only "the man's point of view" or "the woman's point of view." We have had a broader range of experience with our feelings. Though we may be silent about our own feelings when an argument does not directly involve us, we may well be able to identify with both parties.

We are accustomed to speaking aloud about feelings that society considers appropriate for members of our gender, while remaining quiet about our other strong feelings. We can see both sides of an argument because we can *feel* both sides; more exactly, it is without sides for us.

When a gay man listens to a woman talk about her feelings for an important man or woman in her life, he easily identifies with her, just as a lesbian easily identifies with a man talking about the important woman or man in his life. People need constant reminders that *being gay is not a disability, it is an ability*. We are able to act and feel in ways that seem less exclusive to other people in the population, yet we are also quite familiar with "expected" behavior and feelings.

Gays are caricatured as the people who are endlessly entertaining, busy beautifying places and people, and wanting peace because we are afraid to fight. As a group, with our uniquely broader view, we are prone to see the funny sides of things, we do much to create an aesthetic environment that is harmonious with nature, and we work for peace. (This last trait is less a matter of being afraid to fight and more a matter of seeing how silly fighting is.) Love flourishes when savages are tamed or entertained.

It confuses those who do not know us when they see that we have become strident in recent years, demanding the same civil rights as other people. We have taken great risks to demonstrate that we must be treated as equals by the ruling majority. Having found one another in a time of social upheaval, we sense that the time is right for us to show our numbers, unity and strength.

We have the natural right to love in the way that is natural for us. Biologists and ethnographers call us a natural variation in the general population. We are no more exotic than people who have a different color of skin or a different shape of eye.

In many, if not most, areas of the world, sex has been hopelessly complicated by the rules and myths that surround it. We gay people have been especially victimized by the consequent confusion. But we have gained perspective, and it is improving all the time. In a way, it was easier for us. We were told that our homosexual desires were wrong always, under all circumstances, with no exceptions. That did make it easier to see that the morass of rules and complications governing "proper" sexual feelings and behavior was little more than a web that ensnared its weaver. In our hearts we want to bring something positive to one another. Sex can be, and usually is, a very pleasant experience. Like any human interchange, it has its dangers — including the exchange of bacteria and viruses that cause disease. But even these dangers can be overcome unless one has very rigid ideas about a proper way to share sex.

We gay lovemakers are learning, and perhaps others will learn from us, that sex is satisfying when participation or nonparticipation takes into account spiritual needs that are its other side. Human sexuality is no more than a physical function unless it expresses a spiritual bonding. If sex is used to manipulate or exploit someone else, one must live with the consequences of untruthful behavior. Pain comes when you put yourself off balance. The same can be said, by the way, for refusing to engage in some natural physical expression of love when both you and the other person sense that it would be a true opportunity to create love. It is like refusing to offer kindness, consideration, or consolation because you are saving them. No one but you can tell when sex and spirituality are linked and you are ready for lovemaking. And no one but you can dare deny its truth.

This is a time of rapid development for gay people. It is a time in human history when we are aware that we exist in great numbers. The explosion in communication technology allows us to locate one another and compare experience and intuition. We are learning more about ourselves every day.

Happiness is balance. Balance is dependent upon our knowing all that we can know about ourselves. Individually and collectively we must act in the imperfect present as we continue to learn more about ourselves. We have made mistakes and we will continue to make mistakes. The generations that follow need not make the same mistakes.

Even if gays are repressed again, we now have the means to

communicate to one another through the generations. Our situation will never be the same.

If we have learned nothing else, we have learned that it is fine to be the people we are. We are not responsible for having been born as we are. We *are* responsible, however, for making the best possible use of our assets. We are responsible for finding and maintaining our balance. We are responsible for our willingness to receive and give love. We are responsible for accepting happiness and helping others find their way to it.

Every hour, it is our responsibility to be truthful. I must be prepared to tell you when I am sad or angry, or that I desire to share my compassion or my sexuality with you, or that I am not at the moment clear as to what I feel. All statements are equally helpful if they are truthful. Once I have made my own feelings more conscious, other emotions in me will come forward to help me maintain my inner balance. Once I have told another person my feelings truthfully, their responsive feelings will help balance mine. Satisfying behavior will be created from this truthful interchange.

People notice how often we gay people are gentle. It is easier for us to tell our feelings in a gentle, non-demanding way. And it is easier for us to hear the feelings of others in a gentle, accepting manner. It is easier for us because we sense that we have not created the feelings any more than we have created one another. We are not responsible for feelings at all. We are, however, totally responsible for what we do with the feelings.

The world needs us and we need one another. We are lovemakers, caretakers, people who follow a spiritual path, and people who know the necessity of constant change. Our lives have not been easy. We have been edged off balance. But we have found one another now and we are finding our balance. We care for one another and our happiness is larger than life.

Identity

Some people seem to move through life with a serene sense of identity. It is as if they were given a script at birth and they need merely to read their lines and follow the instructions. One of the difficult blessings that comes with being gay is that we must re-define our identities as gay persons throughout our lifetimes. It is a responsibility and a freedom. No one hands us the script. I am not stuck with an identity given to me in the first years of life with prescribed attitudes, values, occupations, desires, and a blueprint for living out my years. I do not have that security, and I am more free to become the person I am.

I do not view being gay today in the way I viewed it ten years ago. The whole world has changed in that time and so have I. We have been riding the crest of a wave of social change in which many of us have had a hard time keeping our balance. Ten years ago I thought that the heart of the matter was having the right to express ourselves sexually and affectionately in a truthful manner. Now I see that while that was a necessary, integral part of our emerging identity, it was only a part.

The one factor that has remained central is our feeling of being different. All of us receive our instructions for self-concept in the form of the language we learn when we are very young. Many languages have a name for the person who is not "one of us," the stranger or the foreigner. In some languages the word implies that the person is a sub-human barbarian.

Because we keep our awareness of feelings that we were instructed to forget, gay people learn early to think of ourselves as the stranger or the foreign person — the one who does not belong and is not fully embraced by family and community. When young, it is experienced as a curse. We have no way of knowing then that it is no worse than being left-handed or having blue eyes.

Thirty years ago, I was a 27-year-old graduate student. I had worked earlier in mental hospitals and I wanted badly to learn the "secrets" of psychology and psychiatry so as to help people find their way out of the confusion that imprisoned them. Of course, I see now that I was trying to find my way out of my own confusion and unhappiness.

One of my clinical courses was taught in the evening by a psychiatrist who seemed to be a knowledgeable and compassionate man. He directed the Insulin Shock Program at a nearby county hospital. As a part of one of my earlier college jobs, I had worked in the shock room of a private hospital that was beautiful on the outside and amazingly ugly inside. The psychiatrist administered electricity to the brains of patients strapped to the table, while a half dozen of us held the violently convulsing body, attempting to prevent broken bones or other traumatic injuries. The doctor in that hospital also made early morning rounds in the shock room, injecting some patients with insulin that induced coma, leaving the frightened, disoriented patients to awaken in a ward tended by unfamiliar nonprofessionals — some of us more understanding and reassuring than others.

But the psychiatrist who taught the course in graduate school seemed to be genuinely humane. He believed that the insulin shock therapy could help. I remember him telling us that, if he had a choice, he would rather that his young daughter develop a psychosis than become neurotic, because then he might be able to help her recover with the aid of an insulin shock program.

One evening the psychiatrist brought with him a patient

from the state hospital. The doctor told us that the two of them would review the patient's case with us and that we could feel at ease about asking questions since the young man was intelligent, well educated, informed about his condition, and articulate in discussing it. The patient also reassured us that he was glad to discuss his case with us if it would help us in our training and, ultimately, help other people.

I do not know how helpful it was for my fellow students but it made a vivid and lasting impression on me. It began in the usual way. "The patient is a Caucasian, well-nourished, 32-year-old male with excellent intellectual functioning. He is well oriented to time and place, with no evidence of organic symptomatology. He has shown no evidence of hallucinations or delusions..."

The patient was a personable, attractive young man dressed neatly in suit and necktie. He seated himself with apparent ease on the table at the front of the classroom. "After talking with several doctors, and at the urging of my family, I admitted myself to the hospital two years ago because of my persistent homosexuality," he said. He was heartbreakingly honest in telling the details of his life. No matter how he had tried to resist his feelings and cooperate with various treatments he had endured, he had failed to find heterosexuality as satisfying as homosexuality. He now accepted the explanation that it was a serious emotional disturbance. The word had not yet come into vogue, but I knew that this man had been brainwashed.

I remember digging my fingernails into the palm of my hand and biting the inside of my cheek so hard that I drew blood. I was afraid that I would cry out involuntarily. I wanted to walk to the front of the room, sit on the table next to him, and tell everyone present that I had the same feelings that he was revealing. In the insane confusion of the moment, I suppose I rationalized that I might yet free myself of the homosexual feelings I had dealt with in psychotherapy some years earlier. I wondered if I needed more treatment. I sat and gripped the arm of my chair.

In my heart, I believe I knew that the only difference between this man and me was that I was more determined and still hoping to conform to the expectations of my society. I had not been found out yet. He was more honest and defeated. I was well on my way to becoming a career doctor; he was well on his way to becoming a career patient. He had been beaten into a kind of genteel submission.

That experience forced me to take another painful step along a path of self-examination that would help me clarify my understanding of myself and other people. Most people are capable of reflection. There are times when we pause and ask of ourselves the most important and difficult question, "Who am I?" It is the quiet ability to ask that question and listen for its answer that makes us human and able to participate in the wonderful process of our own change. It is not always easy.

Last week I sat in my office with a man who cried for ten minutes before he could speak. He has been accurately described as "young, intelligent, friendly, healthy, kind, good-looking, and a real gentleman." He was crying because his best friend had died the day before. His lover had died a month earlier.

When he was able to speak, he said, "I'm not sure I know who I am anymore. Everything's changing too fast." He looked at me with sad, direct eyes. "Are we going to survive this?"

I knew what he meant. "Yes," I answered. "Many of us are dying but we are going to survive and we are going to be stronger and better than we have ever been."

What is it that makes it possible for a person to navigate a stormy period or a whole lifetime of change? How is it possible to keep balance amid currents that change so quickly? In order to maintain stability, one must have a strong sense of identity and the flexibility that is its hallmark.

Many influences contribute to a truthful, strong sense of identity. An awareness of self that comes early in life as a person who is caring and relating — but separate — helps most. Belonging to a family, tribe, nation, or other group whose truthful, strong sense of identity contributes to one's individual sense of identity is another great help.

The subjective experience of change in our lives has become

a large problem. Largely because of technology, our social world is changing at an accelerating rate. It is increasingly difficult to assimilate these social changes. Great stress is produced as people feel they are losing their grasp and are falling behind. Unfortunately this accelerating social change has weakened the identity of the family, tribe, and nation. To add to the misfortune, such social groups are reflexively becoming more rigid because of their fear. There is a desire to cling to the facets of identity that are there no longer. Thus we see people rushing back to the nationalistic fervor and religious customs that served their grandparents well but have little relevance in today's world.

A critical sense of identity, allied with vital flexibility is difficult to maintain today. One is less sure of the answer to the ancient question, "Who are you?" We can answer with an occupation and an address on the planet, but even those are temporary.

Gay people, caught in this contemporary human dilemma, have had something of a head start in finding stability because our answers were so hard-won early in life. Persecuted for the desire to explore and express our love, more and more gay people saw the lie as the current social revolution got under way. Sometimes privately, often publicly, we began to tell the world exactly who we were in terms of thoughts, feelings, and desires that point a direction in life.

It became clear that if a society decreed heterosexuality the only correct form for sexual thoughts, feeling and behavior, that society prized conformity above all. We knew from personal experience that homosexuality and heterosexuality are not neatly categorical. We knew that too much depends upon circumstance, mood, opportunity, and the mysterious attraction that particular individuals have for one another.

Awareness of gay identity comes early in life for most of us. It is not unusual for a gay man to remember awareness of his affection for, and erotic interest in, other males when he was four or five years old. The same is true for a young, developing lesbian.

One man described his feelings for his nineteen-year-old

uncle, experienced when he was five years old. "It was a big family and everybody was busy but Jimmy always had a smile, a kind word, and time for me. Sometimes on Sundays he'd take me swimming out at the quarry. Lots of the kids were scared, but not me. I knew Jimmy would take care of me. Every time I got near him or touched the hair on his arms or smelled him, I'd get this real sweet feeling deep in my stomach. I didn't know it then, of course, but I sure did love him and have a lot of desire for him. All I knew then was that I wanted to go away and live with him somewhere and sleep in the same bed with him as close as possible. Somehow I was smart enough not to tell anybody any of that, though."

Probably that kind of erotic awareness is common to all young people but in parts of the world where it is believed that children should not be erotic, most children try to push such thoughts and feelings away as quickly as possible. But, if the thoughts and feelings are strong, the child is apt to remain conscious of them in an attempt to make sense of them. Survival depends upon one's ability to understand the environment, its rewards and its dangers.

Sooner or later, the person whose erotic attractions are more often homosexual than heterosexual is going to be aware of that fact and try to puzzle it out. It is a difficult job. It is especially difficult when the child trying is surrounded with misinformation.

Gay people eventually settle for the uncomfortable truth. We accept gay identity at the exact time we settle for that truth. Before that, we, like many other people, may have had some homoerotic experiences, and these experiences may have been alarmingly satisfying, but until we have accepted the fact that we are most often attracted to persons of the same gender, we have not accepted a gay identity.

The moment we do assume our gay identity, we begin to see life in a more three-dimensional way. We are not so apt to shy away from perceptions supposedly reserved for "the opposite sex." We can see things from a point of view that is supposedly masculine and at the same time from the point of view that is supposedly feminine. That ability leads to a much richer and fuller grasp of the human experience. It is as if we were using both eyes instead of only one for the first time. The world is viewed in depth. It permits broader understanding and, consequently, a better base from which to anticipate the future. This explains the fact that gay people in various places and times in human history have been shamans or seers, the people who are more able to see what is and what may be.

In some parts of the world we are called *homosexuals*, though the word is more accurately an adjective than a noun. The reason for our society's attaching this name to us seems obvious. We are noticed because of erotic interest in some people of the same gender when official dogma decrees one should have sexual interest in people of the opposite sex only.

Some societies have a fetish for categories. It is obvious that men and women have some anatomical differences as well as some hormonal differences. In truth we are more alike than we are different. But various societies vigorously preserve the myth that men and women are not only different, but opposite. More than likely this has functioned as an effective means of reinforcing the repression of latent homosexual interest and shoring up the sexist dogma that declares women to be second class.

During my college years, I worked for some time in an excellent institution called the Chestnut Lodge Sanitarium. A psychiatrist and personality theorist, Harry Stack Sullivan, had died years before I arrived but his spirit and his theory of interpersonal relations continued to guide the institution. There were rumors among the oldtimers that he had been a homosexual but it was clear that he was loved and "forgiven."

It was his writing that called my attention to the fact that people are more alike than they are different. It had an enormous impact on my thinking. And this thesis of his had an enormous impact on the behavior of the staff. Seriously psychotic patients were treated as individuals who were having an experience we did not quite understand. Our job was to try to understand. Patients were listened to attentively and granted the human dignity that every person deserves. This was far from the style of other mental hospitals of that time.

It may have been that rare humane atmosphere that permitted me to discover that I was falling in love with another male college student who was working there. Our friendship prospered, but not until three years later, in another city, did we find the courage to confess our mutual attraction and love for one another. Such was the repressive and tormented atmosphere of the times. Both of us wanted to put aside these feelings and be "good men." Neither of us wished to harm the other in any way. And so, because our love for one another was strong, it took years to weaken the relationship sufficiently that we could part. We were a minor casualty in a sea of homophobic horror. This was during the time that Joseph McCarthy was involved in the paranoid search for Communists and homosexuals everywhere in the United States.

At Chestnut Lodge I was absorbing the deep lesson that people are more alike than different. Each time I was on the most-disturbed women's ward, I would stop and say a few words to a woman who had been mute and unmoving for years. She would stare into the distance as if not hearing me. One day, as I was about to escort a few of the women from the ward to a dance, I stood waiting, key in the elevator call device, when this woman astonished all of us by quite literally throwing herself at me, landing more or less with arms around my neck and legs around my hips. I was surprised at how big she was. With my studied nineteen-year-old awareness that something important was happening, I looked directly into her eyes and said seriously, "I think you're trying to tell me something, Jeanne."

I worked with her a lot after that. We communicated at first by her checking "yes" and "no" boxes on my scratch pad and a bit later with the first hoarse words she could manage. In a matter of weeks we were able to go on a few outings for picnics, then into town, and finally we took a big trip, by train, to another city to visit her mother. I badly wanted to stay at the Lodge and continue to work with her. Indeed, most of the staff, including Frieda

Fromm-Reichman, the clinical director, wanted me to stay and continue. But the United States Army ruled that an attempted year's leave of absence from college would mean instant induction into the military. My patient became another sad casualty of the times. It seemed that I had no choice. It was the military, jail, or college, but no opportunity to stay and help this person find a second chance at life. It was many years before I realized there had been another option. If it had not been the McCarthy Era and if I had not experienced years of psychotherapy that helped me believe I could make it in the world as a seemingly first-class functional heterosexual, I might have been willing to reveal my homosexual inclinations to the military, endure the branding, and stay where I could do some good.

I had no idea whether this woman who trusted me would have been labeled homosexual, heterosexual, or bisexual, nor did it matter. I understood only that we were more alike than different, though she was an older woman who was a patient in a mental hospital and I was a young man who was a college student trying to make sense of myself and the world. Both of us achieved our dignity as best we could, at some cost, of course, and with little help from society.

Ours is a society that pays lip service to excellence but rewards mediocrity. Average people who fit in with little fuss are made most comfortable. Perhaps we will learn to value difference one day. It is possible to value another person's difference, appreciate it, yet realize that we are more alike than different.

The difference that has set gay people apart in those places in the world that demand heterosexual conformity is, as mentioned earlier, our lovemaking. It is not simple homosexual behavior, per se, that marks a person for persecution. If every person who has acted on homosexual desire once were to be included with the persecuted, the foolishness of the persecution would be seen at once.

The problem is that we are the men who dare to admit we are able and willing to love men, and the women who dare admit to loving women, not in stylized restricted form, but wholly, with all of our being. We spend a small fraction of our lifetimes in sexual intercourse. Gay people usually are not orgasm chasers or sexual conquest addicts, though we have been known to fall into that trap as frequently as our heterosexual peers. A person with a sexual compulsion may prefer heterosexuality or homosexuality. The problem is the compulsion, not the gender of preference.

In 1985 a non-gay colleague confided that he thought gay men had "brought a lot of this disease trouble on themselves because of kinky sexual practices that got way out of control." I had to remind him that we did not invent sex, nor its "kinky" variations. He was particularly concerned about sado-masochistic practices which he had forgotten have long been prevalent in heterosexual society.

I told him that, in my experience, the only difference in people with a predominantly homosexual orientation and those with a predominantly heterosexual orientation is that gay men as a group tend to be more sexually friendly. And that is not surprising, since we have been socially conditioned as men and therefore are expected to attempt multiple contacts. We learned long ago that we could go beyond a handshake (that ancient custom developed to ascertain if another man was carrying a weapon up his sleeve). And in these recent years when we have experienced less need to hide our natural inclinations, we are understandably enthusiastic about showing our interest in one another.

I reminded him also that there are gay men and lesbians who are monogamous and some gay people who are celibate. I advised him that if he was particularly interested in finding a group of people with "kinky" habits that are adhered to by the entire group, he would do better making an anthropological study of some religious sects.

Gay people are just people, though. We deny our sexual interests less than in the past. Most of us have devoted enough of our lifetimes to denial by the time we are a quarter of the way through life. And most of us know that denial of sexual interest and identity has cost too many people their sanity and their lives. My colleague was suffering from an undiagnosed case of myopic homophobia, combined with some tricky thinking left over from religion. The tricky thinking permits the smugly pious to comfort themselves for being physically well while other people are getting sick by assuming that the sick people must have sinned in some way in order to bring such misfortune on themselves. It is not a pretty rationalization.

"You will not deny that it looks as if much of this AIDS disease is sexually transmitted, will you?," he persisted.

I assured him that I would not deny that, and reminded him that many illustrious and well-respected citizens have become ill and many have died from sexually transmitted diseases for centuries, including much of the royalty and certainly several of his favorite eighteenth-century composers of music. The behavior of these people was not particularly "kinky," nor was it necessarily out of control. They simply had the misfortune to contract a disease that was transmitted sexually, for which there was no medical remedy at the time.

Gay people are lovemakers who unnerve their detractors with simple honesty. We admit that we are not average and that we are, by definition, not conformists.

I do not mean to dismiss dissonance easily. There are deep differences at work here. In a society where it is forbidden, consider what it means for a man to have a natural erotic interest in other men. Contrary to popular homophobic belief, such erotic interest does not mean that he will interact sexually with any and all other men who are attractive to him. And, even if that were possible, it is not the heart of the problem.

Erotic interest means one's affectional orientation is loving, protective, emotionally open, and *possibly* sexual. In heterosexually conforming societies a man is expected to have this orientation toward women. It is encouraged and trained. A gay man has received the standard societal training and, though *less often* sexually attracted to women, may have the standard erotic orientation to them. But the gay man has that same orientation to men! He is not suited to be competitive, brutal, and damaging to other men because the erotic orientation predisposes him to be loving, protective, emotionally open, vulnerable, and possibly sexual. The same is true in the gay woman's orientation to other women. Her training disposes her favorably to men but her natural erotic orientation disposes her to intimate closeness (rather than a defensive posture) with other women. The heterosexual-conforming male or female is more available for training by the culture to make him or her compete with other people of the same gender. In our society it is the males who are most actively trained for this competition and combat. This is a real problem that requires our attention. It means that the more heterosexual and conforming a man is, the less able he is (by the time he has been trained to adulthood) to feel collective protective feelings for other males. Without these feelings he is potentially dangerous.

I do not mean to imply that people who by nature are more heterosexual than homosexual ought to be somehow transformed to a more homosexual orientation in order to insure our safety. One must respect a person's true nature. But society does benefit from having some men who are naturally erotic in their orientation to other men, and women who are naturally erotic in their orientation to other women. It provides a sane safety valve, a natural foundation for collective mutual protection in a humane society.

Beyond the general erotic orientation, sexual manifestation in behavior is good also. When it is spontaneous, genuine, and natural, sexuality provides an easy means of bonding. It permits one to be emotionally vulnerable with another human. A society needs men deeply bonded to other men and women deeply bonded to other women if it is to have any chance at peace and collective prosperity based on a societal investment in community well-being.

People are more alike than different, but there *are* differences. Because of our different experience in society, lesbians and gay men are in a position to become more self-aware. We have a good start at answering questions relating to identity. Simple heterosexual conformists cannot help us. They are missing the homoerotic component. But we can help by guiding them in those areas where they cannot see well.

A lesbian friend summed it up nicely. She said, "Look, if you don't know who you are, you're nobody. Just get in line and they'll issue you an I.D., a tv, a meaningless job, and a lifetime supply of stuff that tastes like food. All I can say is thank God for the trouble I cried my eyes out about when I was younger. I tried so hard to be a cheerleader, wife and mother that it makes me sick to remember it. But the truth is that the world lit up only when I touched certain women. I still like men, but I am relieved to know that they can be friends and I don't have to marry one. I don't know all there is to know about who I am, but I know a lot more than most people. I paid the price. And I'm going to find out a lot more about who I am because, no matter what the price is, I'm not going to let anybody turn the lights out on me again!"

A middle-aged gay man who recently came out said, "There's a hell of a storm going on out here, but I'm not about to go back in the closet. That's too lonely a place to ride out any storm."

So grows the determination and strength of true identity and the flexibility that it fosters. With it we keep our balance in storms of change. With it we survive and grow everywhere, even in environments that are unfriendly.

Belonging

Anyone who has noticed that the world is changing has noticed also that the form and function of the family is changing. There still exists a nostalgic sentiment about the large, extended family that was popular and functional at the turn of the century, but it is difficult to find such a family today. There are regional differences on the globe, of course, but even these are disappearing. The world is rapidly becoming more and more homogeneous. And the multigenerational extended family that offered security in exchange for responsibility is vanishing.

We have been trying to make the small, nuclear family do the same job that the large, extended family once did, but it has not succeeded. There are not enough people to share the varied social tasks. One man told me about what he called his traditional American family holiday last year.

"There we were. One mother, one father, one sister, and one brother. It was your basic "happy" family, the one I grew up in. It was Thanksgiving. None of us looked forward to it but we were all determined to be happy. Company would be coming for dinner, as usual, and we were all tense, as usual, and pretending we were relaxed, as usual. My sister was pregnant and without husband, again, and we were not talking about it. My father kept nipping out to the garage for a sip from his hidden bottle, and we were not talking about it. My mother had built a little shrine in the bedroom and would run in there to pray when my father went to the garage and we were not talking about it. It was my first trip home during my freshman year at college, where I had proven to my satisfaction that I am gay, and we were definitely not talking about that. So we told each other how lucky we were to be having such good weather in November."

A slightly happier story about the same holiday was told to me by two lesbians who are lovers. "We had Sue's folks over and my brother and his wife came with their new baby. We had a great time. We all pitched in with the cooking and after dinner a few of our friends stopped by. I would have liked it if my folks had come too, but maybe next year. It's taking them some time to get used to our being a couple."

Conversation about traditional family holidays almost always leads to reminiscing and recognition that families are changing. It is clear that we are trying to get our needs met from families in ways that no longer work. Perhaps no one is more conscious of this than gay people. When there were close extended families, chances were greater of finding someone in the family who knew something about what it meant to be gay. There was a better chance of finding some support.

In the small families of today, parents are more likely to panic at the news of a gay son or a lesbian daughter, to fear that they have done a bad job of parenting, and also to fear that the neighbors will pity or be scornful. The small family unit lacks the perspective to see that this is a natural variation that has long been happening in all families everywhere in the world. Depending upon the time in history and the spiritual maturity of the family, a gay family member might be seen as more or less of a blessing but definitely was not seen as the fault of parents who had not found the right neighborhood, the right schools, the right friends, the right food, and the right television programs.

At best a family can provide a setting that encourages the development of love, and offers emotional support and guidance to its members. Some small family units are able to manage this still, but more are undermined by the doubts and insecurities of individual family members.

And so the way we gather together as social animals continues to change. Various arrangements of tribes, joined families, and family units have evolved over time to meet the needs of individuals in particular circumstances. Our society's small families are not meeting the needs of individuals in these rapidly changing times, and that is the reason new family groupings are emerging. Which of these new forms will prove the most functional and durable we will know only with the passage of time.

But it is worth noticing how this changing phenomenon is manifesting itself amoung gay people. Most have had to give up any pretense of depending upon their biological family as a major source of emotional support. Small families are too dependent upon community approval, and therefore infrequently give the sort of wholehearted emotional support badly needed by a gay person who is "different" and therefore considered undesirable.

While the form and function of the family is changing, the word continues to stay vividly alive in our vocabulary. That gives a clue to what is missing. Something the family used to offer is still badly needed.

Less and less often do I hear a lesbian or gay man speak of their family as such. Reference is made to one's mother, father, brother, sister, niece, nephew, cousin, uncle, or aunt, but seldom "my family." It is clear that the speaker is making reference to someone from the original biological family. But rarely does the gay person speak of "my family" as if it were a unit that could be contacted. The individuals to whom one is biologically related are there, some more emotionally close than others, but the group as a unit is losing life.

By contrast, I often hear a friend described in such emotionally protective and appreciative terms that it is clear this is a special friend. Oh, Jane! She's *family*." Among gay people additional information is welcome but not required. We know what that means. This person is a friend who is meeting needs that used to be met by families.

It is not unusual for a gay man or a lesbian to have an interesting network of family. Each of us started out in some sort of biological family. More often than not there is some degree of estrangement because it has been difficult for the gay person to tell the whole truth and for the family to hear the whole truth. Often there is some sort of truce while the form of family relationships continue. There are phone calls or letters but the most complex feelings and urgent changes in life are either not discussed or are glossed over. That is sad. Even if the small family unit cannot meet its mythic responsibility, it is too bad the individuals involved are unable to keep real love alive and must rely on the emptiness of duty. It is impressive to me that the lesbian or gay male offspring are more often tolerant and understanding of idiosyncracies of parents and siblings than these people are able or willing to be with them.

Today, there is the phenomenon of interim families. (This phenomenon is not restricted to gay people, of course. Adolescents lean more and more on peers for support and assume a lack of understanding and support in their biological families. It helps in the move from dependency into an unknowable future.) The interim family seems to be a temporary phenomenon for the non-gay person emerging from the family shell. They have a general idea of the forms their lives are to take. They know they are to look for a mate, have children, and resume altered relationships with family members. Everyone has read the script and seen it acted out countless times with endless variations.

For the gay person, whose family often is not fully emotionally available, and who will not follow the track of marriage, children, and grandchildren, the interim family becomes very important. There is more affection felt and shown. The interim family is used to learn about people and make careful choices of friends. Everyone in the interim family is changing, and learning from one another's changes. There is a greater unspoken demand that members of the interim family take responsibility for one another and be clear in the offering of the love, emotional support, guidance, and encouragement one hopes to find in a family.

As is true in non-gay interim families, there is a lot of helping one another through first romances and broken hearts that are truly painful. A unique feature that surprises non-gay people about these interim gay families is that the former lover who was the seeming cause of the heartbreak often becomes a very close lifetime friend. The ex-lover, more often than not, becomes "family." We need one another.

Life teaches us all the same lessons during our growing up years. It demands that we learn the ways of the world as best we can and make provision for an unknowable future. Develop your strengths, become as self-sufficient as you are able, and be aware of the people who will help you get through the difficult times.

Since gay people cannot rely on the usual family and community supports, we look to one another and we look carefully. Non-gay observers think it odd that two lesbians or two gay men who form what seems to them to be a reliable bond are usually so eager to find a home and move in together. Of course, we are only people, and have to learn from mistakes like everyone else. So we see a lot of moving in and moving out again. With experience, most of us learn to take it a bit easier and let the courtship run a natural, slower course.

For us, "dating someone" usually means you have met someone you think may be your special mate but you are trying to keep your options open by seeing other people. It is a way of guarding against a broken heart. It is comparable to the non-gay person who says "I've been out on quite a few dates with him."

Then "seeing someone" moves into a second, more serious, phase when it is understood that the two people will spend several nights a week together and be together on all important social occasions unless an unusual circumstance prevents it. It is comparable to the conventional engagement.

For us, marriage comes most often when the two people move into a home together. That housewarming party is a wedding party and every guest who is gay knows it. Gay friends and gay family come with their blessings and hopes for a good future. It is the beginning of a new family unit.

And that is why, though we may learn restraint, there is often an eager hope to move in together soon. If it is the right person, the mate for life, it means that you have found your own family at last. Your insecure period in limbo is finished. You know who will offer sympathy, help, and encouragement when you need it. You know who will place your welfare on the same level as his or her own. And you know who trusts you and loves you enough to count on you for the same security.

Understanding this helps to explain the mystery about why biological family members are so often reluctant to appear at the housewarming celebration. They may have ready excuses about other plans and determinedly not see a housewarming as such a special event but, consciously or not, they know this is as important as any wedding. They are withholding their blessing. To bless the event and wish the future happiness of the couple would be to admit that their community-based prejudice and lack of support has been wrong. It is guilt that keeps the non-gay family member from the generous gift of celebration.

As is true when any two people marry, there is a period of sorting biological relatives and friends to see who will be close and supportive. For the gay couple establishing their home and life together, the sorting is more important. There continue to be more than enough forces in the community that deny the validity of their love for one another and act overtly or covertly to separate the two people. The newly forming family must be composed of people who support the union and wish the best for both people. A few siblings make it into this new family, but few parents do. The wall of guilt and blame, often unspoken, that has been building for years is now firmly in place. Quite often the relationship with the parent will now fade to the phone call in which the parent may muster the courage to ask, "And how is your friend?"

Among both gay people and non-gay people, there are more at any given moment who are single than there are in a committed relationship. But the peculiar circumstances surrounding adolescent and early adult years for the gay person has laid a groundwork for what may be a very fundamental kind of family that may better tend the needs of those who are not yet married, widowed, or between engagements.

This new family is a family of choice. The people in it choose one another. Rarely are there announcements of ceremonies, it seems to just happen over time. It is the continuation of earlier dynamics. It started with lonely gay individuals learning to find those who would be genuine and appreciative in receiving the love being offered and who were unselfish and reliably trustworthy in giving their own love in response. More often than not, the gay person's family of choice contains a few very appreciated non-gay people.

These families of choice, for whatever reason, seem to have taken root most heartily in the baby-boom generation. Perhaps it was because they grew up in one of the few times when the world thought there was a genuine chance of peace and brotherhood. The world was becoming rapidly smaller and these people, as children, knew their future adult neighbors would be people their parents' generation saw as foreigners. Or maybe it is simply because there are so many of them, born out of the ruins of war. For whatever reason the gay people of that generation have done a splendid job of reaching out to one another.

The words "we are a family" evoke emotion easily. Some people react to the words with deep stirrings of love, some with scorn, some with real hatred, but few people are unaffected. The words reach deep into our need to be loved and cared for, to feel secure, and to have our love and caring valued.

Hundreds of times I have heard gay men and lesbians talk about how odd relationships were within their families. Too often they felt that their loving did not work right, somehow. There seemed to be a clumsiness in the expression of affection with parents. They felt they were doing something wrong, sometimes being too demonstrative, sometimes too undemonstrative. As one man told me, "It seemed that every time I approached either of my parents I had too many elbows and knees, my head was in the wrong position, and the lap was never where I was expecting it to be." The problem probably has something to do with parental expectations of how boys and girls should express affection to mothers and fathers. There are latent sex-role expectations always.

A lesbian friend said, "I really loved the way my mother looked, smelled and felt. But by the time I was about nine years old, it seemed as if every time I approached my mother it reminded her that she had to go shopping, start dinner, or vacuum the living room rug. I remember wondering if there was something wrong with her. Then, of course, I decided it must be something wrong with me." The corollary is the very frequently told story of the boy reaching for his father's hand on the street, usually at about age six, then feeling rebuked and hurt when the father's hand is withdrawn and put in a pocket.

For a gay child, whose affectional-erotic preference is well established by these ages, it is an awakening of sorts. Though the parent may remember the awkwardness in later years and wonder what the problem was, the child gets the message: Hold back on your natural urges to share love, affection and body contact. It is difficult for a child to hold back and store those urges. Such inhibition is unnatural. Should she find a teacher, older relative, or family friend who is especially fond of the child and welcomes the affectionate contact, the child is apt to let the stored need loose and frighten off this next adult with a vague sense that it is somehow "too much." The lesson is reinforced: Hold back on your natural urges to share love, affection and body contact.

When the gay person finally makes contact with gay peers, he sometimes finds it difficult to let loose of the old inhibitions, and let out the feelings that have been stored away, for many years. The need to care for someone and to feel cared for, to share love, affection, and body contact, is strong. It is the stored need to bring love and make love.

We gay people are apt to be shy when we begin to find one another. Role models have usually been unavailable and we are not sure how to go about making gay friends and expressing our feelings. We are forced to find ways to help one another "come out" and to welcome feelings that have been in hiding.

We look for the same virtues in the family of choice that anyone would want if they could select their family. We look for people who share our values and interests. We look for people we consider admirable, trustworthy, reliable and honest. There is pressure within the gay community to develop these characteristics if you hope to develop a family of choice.

The transition from the non-gay world and the biological family to this new world can be confusing. All groups have their training grounds, and the gay sub-culture is no different. I remember the first awful months in the military service when it seemed that every person who had failed in all other aspects of life, but had been in the military longer than I, rushed to give me the true answers on how to get along in that new world. I had to sort their suggestions and find my own way. The person new to the gay sub-culture is exposed to the same eager guides, and must sort and find his or her way too. In the confusion of the training period, one is usually taken advantage of one way or another, one time or another. But we learn. And the people who give us bad information and take advantage of us do not become our friends.

We are a community much like any other. We have our failures, those who are dishonest, poorly informed, have an inflated opinion of themselves, or who will gladly take advantage of another person. The difference is that we have been hurt in our invisibility while growing up and, as a group, have developed more compassion for others like ourselves. And we are lonely for family. Our families of origin may not have been perfect but they gave more comfort to other members of the family than we were able to find. We did not quite belong. Once out in the world we are eager to find family. And this time around, we are looking for real family, not one in name only.

The family of choice that evolves is almost always an integrated one. It is composed of those people who are gay and have become family, those people found along the way who are not gay

but have become family, and those to whom one is biologically related who have come through and learned to appreciate you
because you are gay, not in spite of that fact. They are not always
parents, brothers or sisters, but there are usually at least one or
two who are blood relatives.

The AIDS epidemic has helped us get life in perspective in
many ways. Like other people, we realized how much of life we
were wasting, diverting ourselves in silly ways and looking for
perfection in the wrong places. In coming to terms with death, we
learned a lot about living. This is what happens invariably when
one is forced to live in the present and be honest. Among the
things we learned was that we could build even better families of
choice.

I think of one man who was single and past fifty years old.
He had had a few brief romances in his life, but had made up his
mind that he was too old for a relationship and would have to live
out his remaining days as a lonely person. He was intelligent
enough to recognize it as the very prophecy he had been given
when he announced to his family of origin that he was gay. But he
saw no alternative.

The health crisis mobilized him. He found the time and
energy to care for those who needed care and they appreciated
him just the way he was. He told me that the experience taught
him the necessity of being honest no matter how difficult. He
learned that his honesty was invariably rewarded. It was hard for
him to admit to others that he was lonely; he had made his peace
with life as a single man. "In fact, I rather liked my life, even if it
had become a bit routine," he told me. "Most difficult was that I
hated facing that bed alone all the time. Oh, most nights it was
perfectly fine, but it was the knowing that I was doomed to sleep
alone *every* night."

He confessed this to a young man who was a fellow volunteer. The young man asked if he were talking about sex or a bed
companion. He realized that he meant both. "I told him that after
all I am a healthy gay male and could certainly use a bit of healthy
gay sex now and then. But, every bit as important, I wished there

were friends I could just share sleep with, maybe cuddle, and have the feelings reciprocal."

His wish was granted, of course. He found several friends who, like himself, enjoyed sleeping cuddled up with someone they cared for and trusted. "It's improved my life *and* my friendships," he said. "They're family now. We can roll out of bed for morning coffee and not have to look any better than we do. We like one another because we are the people we are. And, amazingly enough, sex has begun to find its way to me once again too." The problem was that he had given up on the idea that he was desired. And perhaps he was less attractive as he led his rigid life, looking into a bleak future.

It was this same man who told me that he had been aware for many years that he had family that spoke to him across the generations with the music they wrote, the buildings they built, and the books they left. He felt related to them, loved them, and mourned them. Yet he had not considered the possibility that they also existed *now*, in his city. He had not yet heard their music, seen their buildings, read their books. He had not thought in recent years simply to reach out and meet a stranger honestly, person to person. He found people who were older, younger, more and less affluent, more and less physically attractive, and more and less able to articulate their feelings. But he found them because he dared to be honest about himself and his needs, not pleading as a beggar but bringing the gift of himself to those who found him of value.

A lesbian friend wrote in a letter, "You're born alone and you die alone, but there's no law that says you have to sleep alone. I went through a whole winter when I thought I was pregnant because I had this awful feeling in my stomach. I slept wrapped around a pillow every night. Finally it got to be so silly that I even went to see my doctor to find out if I *was* pregnant — though it would have been an immaculate conception as far as I knew. She took me into her office, sat me down, and said 'You're a lonely lady and a good person. I prescribe one or two other ladies who are good people. It doesn't have to offend your sense of morality.

Think of it as being thirteen years old and having a slumber party.' She was right. It was vulnerability. And her prescription worked. I think we'd better reorganize the old folks' homes. Sleeping alone all the time cannot possibly be healthy."

As I have watched, the direction that gay families of choice seem to be taking in recent years looks functionally adaptive for a future that can never be predicted. We seem to be picking up the best of what family has had to offer and leaving that which is no longer relevant. Gay families of choice rarely live in big sprawling mansions (though there are some of those), and almost never live in boxy little tract houses. A few years back such families tended to be homogeneous in age, but that seems to be changing now too.

Lesbians and gay men who were once heterosexually married often bring sons and daughters into their gay families. Some decided to adopt young children and some, more recently, are conceiving and giving birth through artificial insemination. As new babies entered gay families the realization came naturally that it is a wonderful comfort not only to watch children grow but also to lean on the love, wisdom, and experience of elders as you help them finish out their final years with the greatest possible dignity. It is not so unusual now for a gay family of choice to range in age from one month to more than eighty years.

One man who is nearing forty years of age said, "I feel sorry for people in my parents' generation. Most of them got stuck raising kids who left an empty nest. And now they're having to pay to keep their own parents in expensive nursing homes. And by some magic of fate, I'm enjoying what their parents were nostalgic for. It's the big extended family all over again. We still need nursing homes and nursery schools but my lover and I have plenty of babysitters for our two-year-old. Her favorite, of course, is our 79-year-old lesbian friend who loves to read to her. Our little one can't understand a word, but she must get the feeling, because she sure likes to sit in her Grandma's lap and be read to." A good family nurtures all its members.

The task of a lovemaker is to bring love as an offering, and with that as a start to make more love than there was before. We are redefining the concept of belonging and family for ourselves. We are making it work again. Maybe, as has been suggested by some people, we are reinventing the wheel. Or maybe we are the ones who remembered that it is round, fashioned with care, and can easily carry more than its own weight.

Recognition

Recognition is a kind of awakening. *Cognition* is the word used to describe our perceiving, thinking and sensing; the way we process incoming information so that we can grasp or "know." When we *re*-cognize, it is usually because new information helps us to call up something already known and see it in a new light. Recognition implies a truer knowing. We meet someone on the street whom we have not seen for a while, assimilate whatever has changed in appearance, and *recognize* the person. We face some truth that we have been avoiding, assimilate it, and *recognize* the more true state of affairs in our personal world.

I met a man on the street a few months ago who had been a student when I was a college professor. We laughed to find one another so changed in appearance, yet somehow still identifiable as the same persons. I remembered him with pony tail and beads, playing his guitar in the library that was barricaded as part of a student anti-war demonstration. Now he was wearing a navy three-piece suit, carrying a slim leather briefcase, and sporting an elegant hair style. "You've changed!" I said, glad to see him and stating the obvious.

"What can I tell you?" he said. "I was a revolutionary! Then I was the ghetto schoolteacher, then the computer whiz-kid, and now I'm a stockbroker. Who knows what next? Of course, along the way, you may remember I came out to myself, then to you, then to other people; I marched in the parades, carried the banners, and now I have to come out all over again. Only a few of my friends back in New York know about this new life. Can you imagine the reactions I'm going to get?"

I was able to recognize my former student because his face and eyes were familiar to me and I made a quick adjustment to his new costume. I had to do some reorganizing in my mind in order to recognize him, just as he had to do to recognize me with my graying hair and glasses. It is impressive how quickly the human mind is able to reassemble incoming data so that recognition can happen.

While the recognition process goes on constantly for all of us, there is a pattern of major awakenings or major recognitions that is familiar to most adult gay men and lesbians today. The first awakening often happens when the person is very young. It involves a sudden involuntary awareness, or recognition, that you are alone. Perhaps this happens to everyone, but most people soon put it aside. For gay people it is a building block essential to future growth.

When I was four years old, my family lived in Florida for a year. My moment of recognition, or awareness, happened during that year. It came near midday while I was digging in the sandy yard not far from the house we were renting. I remember that the sun felt very warm and I was looking at the depth of the hole I was digging. I was wondering just how deep I could dig, since the sand kept slipping back into the hole. For no obvious reason, I stopped both my digging and my contemplation quite abruptly. I became aware of the quiet, my kneeling position, what I was wearing, the warmth and stillness of the air, and the lack of visible people in my surroundings. I was alone. I knew there were people nearby. But it was the first time I was aware that I was *separate*, not attached to anyone. I was a self. I did not know much about myself, but I knew something I had not known clearly before. I was an individual, a separate person. From that moment, I began consciously to wonder who I was and tried to find out more about myself. I have heard similar stories from hundreds of gay men and women.

One woman said, "I came to life while I was getting a haircut. The feeling was like 'What the hell is going on here? They're cutting off parts of me and I'm not sure I like it. The haircutter was chatting it up with my mom and I thought, 'Okay, girl, you're in this alone. Pay attention.' I think that was my first real coming out. It was a beginning. I came out to myself as a person, not just an appendage to my mom."

Perhaps after that first "coming out" we are more alert than other children. Every child struggles with the conflict between inner feelings and the commands of the surrounding world. We have all heard an adult voice that says, "No. Now you put that down. That's not your toy, it's hers. You have your own toys at home." It seems that it ought to be all right just to pick up the desired toy and run, but when the adults who police the world tell us it is wrong, we have to make our peace with their ruling.

All of us are also familiar with the adult voice that says to the angry child, "Now behave. You need a nap." It is a demand to forget the emotion that you are presently feeling because it has been judged "wrong".

Perhaps gay children remain more alert to the rules of their environment because of what we are *not* told. Very early in life, our strong loving feelings, male for male, and female for female, are discouraged. Adults try to redirect these feelings as they did with our anger. "You're too old to kiss another boy now. Here, shake his hand like this," he is told. "You mustn't touch Aunt Betsy's breast. That's for babies. When you're older, you'll have breasts too," she is told. A child cannot begin to understand what these feelings have to do with age.

The earliest remembered time in life when self-esteem is undermined often is connected with being told that there is something "wrong" about our loving feelings and desires. The implication is that we are wrong and bad for having our feelings and desires. The damage begins.

But the feelings persist with no encouragement and despite strong discouragement. We arrange our behavior as much as possible to conceal these feelings and we hope for the best. As we remain alert to incoming data, all of the news about our loving feelings seems to be bad. And still the feelings do not go away. We learn the appropriate behavior for little gentlemen and little ladies and still these feelings do not go away.

The second major awakening — recognition, or "coming out" to oneself — happens when we are consciously confronted with the basic facts of our nature. They had been hiding from full awareness, though there were glimpses of their truth earlier. The realization born of this recognition is brief and usually unpleasant: "Am I really one of those?"

A friend told me it happened to him when he was a senior in high school. "God knows, I held off from recognizing it as long as I could, but then it happened. I had an old tin can of a car and I had just dropped my date off and was on my way home late at night. I was hoping my Dad wouldn't yell at me. I had passed a guy about my own age hitchhiking and I wondered if he had missed the last bus. The light took forever to change. I wondered if I should turn around and pick the guy up — sort of a good deed. The light still didn't turn green. Then I realized I was imagining driving the guy home and kissing him goodnight and the thought was more exciting than the kiss I had just given my date. The light turned green outside and inside my own mind at the same time. 'Oh, Christ,' I thought. 'I'm a goddamned *homo*.' Not a very flattering way to welcome myself."

After this awakening, the second major recognition of self, many of us redouble our defenses and determine not to be found out while we study the matter further. This is a tormented period for most of us, when we try hard to conform and try harder to have the feelings we are told we are supposed to have. It is a time during which self-esteem is further damaged. We hear others talk about "people like that" in the most unflattering ways while we keep our identity invisible, listen, and sometimes pretend to agree. Except for the fortunate few of us who are able to accept their identity easily, this is a time of hard struggle.

A black social worker I know told me that she landed in Juvenile Hall three times during this period of her life. "My poor parents had no idea what was going on. I was so scared and so angry I didn't know which way to turn, and Juvie was better than people finding out. I considered church, but those socials and Bible reading were for my parents' generation. If I thought anybody was looking·at me the wrong way, I hit first and asked questions later. Even the boys were scared of me. I figured a few of them had me pegged as a dyke, but at least they were too afraid of me to say it out loud." She later learned that her brother, who was two years older, was gay also, and had been slugging it out in the same neighborhood for the same reasons. "We all thought he was on his way to being a prize fighter. I had no idea it was all bluff. In fact, he can't stand getting hit."

The third major awakening comes with the recognition that continued hiding of the true self is too costly in self-esteem. Often it has begun to adversely affect the person's emotional and physical health in noticeable ways. The time is ripe to "come out" and salvage self-respect.

A lot has been written about the experience of disclosure. It is always a vivid, often traumatic, experience in the life of a lesbian or gay man. But most of us do reach that point when we realize that some of the most important relationships in our lives are a lie. Not infrequently, youngsters have walled themselves off from bewildered parents, presenting a proper facade, confiding nothing. Close friends are given only the information we believe they can tolerate. We come to see that these people who say they love us do not know us. There is a facet of our being that is so important that we do not go one day of our life without worrying about it, and it is a secret.

Naturally, having been invisible, and therefore privy to the insulting things that parents and friends routinely say about gay people, we expect the worst possible reaction. We expect that they will care for us less and not want to have anything more to do with us once they find out about our loving, homoerotic inclinations. And often parents or friends fulfill that expectation. Some people do sacrifice a son, daughter, or best friend on an altar of homophobic prejudice. As more gay people become visible and there is more information available through books and films, this deeply ingrained prejudice is slowly fading. But the gay person about to make the identity disclosure always takes a dreadful chance — and knows it.

Sometimes the disclosure is held off for fear that the information will kill a parent with a bad heart, or because "my friend has had too many shocks this year," or with a rationalization such as "why not let my parents enjoy their old age in peace?" But the truth does not go away. We know that if someone loves the two-dimensional person we have presented to them, they do not love us. They cannot love us unless they know who we are — all of the important facets of us, including our gay identity. Unlike other people, we must risk the relationships we trust and most value, fearing that if we reveal our true self we will be hated, loathed, pitied, hurt, and possibly banished.

This disclosure is a presentation of one's true identity to other persons. It is the statement, "I am gay." Three little words. We always hope for three words in return: "I love you." But we know we risk the end of a valued relationship.

This third major awakening and recognition is followed by a period of reorganization in the gay person's life. Some people have an immediate, positive reaction to the disclosure that is interlaced with plentiful reassurance. But this may be followed by increasing coolness and distance. Every person who is gay has had this experience. "He told me it didn't make any difference at all and that he only wished he had known earlier because he hated to think of me carrying that secret alone. We had dinner two days later and things were almost the same but a bit different. I tried to bring it up but he brushed it off by saying he had already told me it didn't make any difference. That should have been my clue, I guess. Then he went out of town for two weeks. Then we spent a month not being able to find a time when we could get together for lunch or dinner. And that's the last I've seen of him for six years. I guess it did matter. And I guess he was never my friend. "

A very typical story is for one parent (often the mother) to take the news relatively calmly, while the other parent seems unable to cope with the new vision of son or daughter. Very often, time heals, and the family is reunited with more genuine affection than before. Sometimes not. Being a parent helps most people mature, but not all. The parents who have the greatest trouble dealing with the disclosure are the ones who have a desperate personal need to depend upon their own fantasy pictures of their child as a prop for sagging self-esteem. They do not know what it means to be a loving parent to a real person whom they cannot control or mold.

Disclosure permits important people in your life to re-organize their understanding of you, and thus recognize you. It also permits you to re-organize your understanding of these important people and recognize them anew. A patient told me, "I always thought my old man was a turkey. I thought he was incapable of a new thought. I thought he watched old movies on tv because he couldn't handle anything new. But I gave him the news anyway, and he turned around so fast I didn't know what was happening. All of a sudden he wants to know what a gay person would think about a book that he read or he wants to know if I had any boyfriends when I was in high school. Last night he called me and asked me if he had ever done anything to hurt my lover before he knew he was my lover. I can't believe it. It's like he's making up for lost time as a father. I have to get used to having a father all of a sudden."

Some of this reorganization period involves mourning. The disclosure represents change — important change. The way people who are important in your life respond to more knowledge about you naturally changes your feelings about them too. You lose some people and gain more closeness with others. It is a crucial turning point in life that people who are not gay have a difficult time understanding.

Children play hiding games because they want to be found. The fun is the excitement of anticipating that you will be brought back again, safe and wanted. The cleverer the hiding place, the longer you can enjoy the anticipation of being found.

When it is not a game, however, hiding is a terrible experience. People hide for fear of real or imagined danger. You do not anticipate being welcomed when found. You dread being found and fear the punishment of being exposed.

We gay people learn to hide with good reason. We are given a clear message all our lives that we will not be acceptable to the community if this fact of our life is exposed. We know that people are willing and able to cause us physical and emotional harm if they find us.

There is no rational reason to explain the reactions of the world that surrounds us. But it is clear that they are afraid of us simply because they do not know us. Most of us are invisible to them. We are told ugly myths about ourselves and threatened by many of the same people who say they love us.

And so we climb into the misery of our hiding place, deep within ourselves. We go through the motions of life, studying how other people look and behave, trying to look and behave as they do. We absorb ourselves in creating a false exterior.

Today we have experienced enough freedom to be able to abandon some of the most obvious stereotypes. We learn that lesbians don't have to be mean and tough caricatures of macho masculinity. We know that gay men do not have to have limp wrists, or lisp, or communicate only superficial gossip. But, once free of the most obvious sterotypes, how is the hidden person to present herself to the world? After a lifetime of assuming that my inner self is ugly, it would be bizarre to imagine exposing it undefended to the world.

What often happens is that, like certain poorly defended creatures in the sea, we find other discarded shells that fit better but still hide and protect us. The middle-class gay man may dress himself in a blue-collar outfit, complete with workboots. The lesbian may buy a dress with a plunging neckline if that is new for her. We are like children pulling costumes from the dress-up chest to see how we feel in various images. We want to see a pleasing image reflected in others' eyes, because we are not yet ready to expose the self in hiding.

Having found others of our own kind, we are ready to chant "Come out, come out, wherever you are" but we are not quite ready to chant "Come out, come out, *whoever* you are!" lest someone make the same demand of us. We know that, with the right disguise, we can announce that we are gay and some gay people will accept and even appreciate us. We do not have a clue as to what their reactions would be if they saw the hidden person of whom we think so poorly but know so little of ourselves.

Throughout the centuries, sages have advised us to know ourselves. The advice is as good today as ever. It is essential for the lesbian and gay man. We cannot live our lives until the self is discovered. As long as the self is in hiding or in disguise, we cannot know it.

In order to provide sufficient safety for the inner being to show itself, we must learn the art of self-recognition. It is an ongoing process. It involves being willing to take a fresh look, question old assumptions, gather new information, and accept the evidence in order to re-think and re-perceive the inner reality. We must remember that our misguided sense of reality began when we were very young, without suspicion that our perception of ourselves and people like us was being distorted by a heavy diet of misinformation.

We must also learn that a very possible answer to a simple, searching question is, "I don't know." It is often the most honest answer. You cannot know until you know. You can only be willing to know.

As the new re-cognition of self gets under way, you find yourself looking at other people and the world with more understanding, compassion and appreciation. The dead wood is being cleared away and you begin to see what is there, almost as clearly as you once did when you were a very young child — before you were told what to think and what to believe. It is an amazing experience to begin to trust yourself, your own thinking, and your own perceptions. There is less fear of yourself and others. It becomes less necessary to try to change others because you see their temporary need for their own defenses.

After we step honestly into the world, the healing of self-esteem begins. We begin to realize that we must accept what comes in life and deal with it as honestly as possible. It is a path of less resistance to truth. We must learn to accept reality as it is at the moment. We have learned firsthand how senseless and unprofitable it is for people to refuse to accept us *as is*.

The first three major awakenings have become an expected part of the path for the gay man and lesbian. The major recognitions or awakenings that follow are a newer phenomenon, a part of these fast changing times. They have been experienced already by many gay individuals in recent years. They represent a newer collective gay awakening that has been hastened by the AIDS crisis.

The first of these recognitions is an awareness of our nature as lovemakers, an awakening as to who we are that is quite different than who we have been taught to believe we are. Mythology tells us of the phoenix rising from the ashes. Good is apt to be born from any tragedy if we permit it. Not only did the coming of the AIDS crisis hasten the healing recognition of ourselves as lovemakers, but that recognition now is quickly followed by subsequent awakenings. These have to do with our role as caretakers, our spirituality, and our special ability to cooperate with life change.

In the early days and years of our lives, we gay men and lesbians had loving feelings of attraction to particular people, some of whom were of our own gender. That is probably true for all human babies and infants. Humans vary in the intensity of every trait and talent present early in life. Our feelings of attraction to people of the other gender were no problem. But, unlike the majority of our peers, as we grew older the strength of our attraction to some people of the same gender was too strong to be driven from awareness forever by societal decree and social pressure.

Our loving feelings, attractions, and desires were an essential part of who we were, too strong to be denied. A society may prefer people who are blond, blue-eyed, right-handed, tall, and light-skinned. But if you are brunette, brown-eyed, left-handed, short, and dark-skinned, that is who you are. No matter how hard you try to conform to the desired image, you will fail to be that person.

Society attempts to rationalize irrational preferences. People who are left-handed may be said to have the Devil within. People with dark skin may be said to be stupid and lazy. People who are short and have dark eyes may be said to be sly, crafty and selfish.

Gay people in many contemporary societies were put in an elegantly crafted "no-win" situation. We young males, unable to deny our loving feelings of attraction to some other males, and young females, unable to deny loving feelings of attraction to some other females, because of the durable strength or integrity of these feelings, were told we were "homosexuals." Focus was on the *sexual* aspect of our natural desire to express our loving feelings. And we were taught that homosexuality is sinful and illegal.

It is clever torture. Most people can control their sexual behavior most of the time. But we humans cannot control our feelings. If I feel lovingly attracted to another man, I feel a whole array of loving feelings and desires. It would be natural for some of these feelings to be sexual with some men. But if I have been trained to focus all of these feelings into sex and told that I must never express those sexual feelings, my life will soon be dominated by severe sexual conflict that will make me very unhappy. I will not think then about how I appreciate an attractive man's good qualities and enjoy his company. Instead, I will be focused on my own conflicted sexual desire.

Most gay people grow up with a vague feeling that they are "wrong" and unwanted. The cause of this feeling is not mysterious. It has been made clear to them that men who love men and women who love women are undesirable in the community. By the time we recognize our strong attraction to some people of the same gender, we have been taught that the attraction means that we have an odious, insatiable desire for a *wrong kind* of sexual experience.

And so we fight our feelings until their focused strength is too strong, and then we become "the homosexual" who (naturally) tries to feel wanted and desired by other homosexuals, since being wanted and desired in the larger community seems to have been ruled out by the admission of same-gender attraction. This reinforces the heavy emphasis on sexual desirability.

But many of us now recognize we are far more than sexual animals. Our desire to express our loving feelings, sexually or not, with others of the same gender was discouraged and held back. We were taught to think of ourselves as unwanted, undesired, and undesirable people. We were confused by the emphasis on sex in our learned self-image. What we really have in common with other gay people is the awareness of feelings of love and desire for some people of the same gender.

We may have been taught to seek affirmation of our worth by being sexually desirable. But now we understand that our worth is not to be found in sexual acts. Sex, like any human interaction, can be bad or good, depending on circumstance and motivation.

We recognize now that our worth is to be found in exercising our very strong need to give our love and to receive love. It is the exact facet of our nature for which we have been persecuted. The integrity of this need has cost us more than most people can understand. We need not fight our true feelings any longer. We can embrace them now with pride. We have earned the right to call ourselves lovemakers. We create love. We have fought clear of the confusion that tortured us. We have sexual needs, as do all people. Our loving includes and goes beyond our sexual needs. It has caused us to develop our potential as human caretakers and tenders. It is leading us to the discovery of our own spirituality. And it has taught us the valuable secret of human ability to cooperate with change.

Part Two

CARING

Natural Tenders

In parts of the world where love and sex have become confused and confusing, it is not surprising that we gay people are noticed and disapproved of because of our lovemaking. Our lovemaking is unusual, different from the prescribed variety, and it therefore makes conforming citizens uncomfortable.

We also are noticed because of our caretaking. It is another facet of human interaction that is confused, creates emotional conflict, and therefore is confusing in this part of the world. Like our lovemaking, our caretaking is often different, therefore non-conforming, and once again it makes conforming citizens uncomfortable.

Societies like ours train people to be aggressive and competitive. Aggression is woven into the moral fabric of the society. Reminders of it flash across our television screens and fill our newspapers, thereby reinforcing what we have been taught. Winning is good and losing is bad. Competition is interesting. Recitation of appreciation and description of reality are boring.

Compassion and awareness of human interdependence are a less intense part of our emotional makeup today. If there is a toxic leak in a chemical plant that kills and maims thousands of people, vivid depictions of the event are immediately flashed around the planet. The intensity of our emotional response is dimmed by the daily witnessing of tragedies in this consumer fashion. There is some compassion. We feel sorry for the victims. But our interest shifts to the rules of the game. How responsible are the owners and managers of the plant where the disaster happened? How much money should be paid to the victims? Under what set of rules should the decisions be made? The tragedy has happened. Now, who will win most in the ensuing contest?

A bomb explodes in a crowded airport or railway station. People are killed and maimed. We see pictures of it happening, hear the screams and cries, read the descriptions. We feel sorry for the victims. But attention shifts to the rules of the game. Who should be punished and how? Can we take some of their lives and property without losing more ourselves? In this shrinking world of competing ideologies, what new rules of the game do we need? How is it to be decided when one side or the other has won?

Real human tragedy has become an everyday event. The victims are losers. We feel sorry for them briefly and hope to avoid their fate with luck or cunning. Our compassion is fleeting. Awareness of the interdependence of humans in community is dimmed by the awesome hint that we now live in a community the size of the planet rather than the town or city of a hundred years past. The human mind is making its developmental adjustment more slowly than the advances of technology that have plunged us suddenly into this expanded community.

Today surprise comes not in response to vivid human tragedy around the world, but when natural human compassion and awareness of human interdependence rise to the surface in response to that tragedy. We are pleased and surprised when we revert to the spontaneous impulse to help one another or care for one another. We are moved when we see evidence that reminds us that we must help one another or no one wins.

There is an earthquake that severely damages a city, killing people, destroying property, and trapping survivors. Volunteers, locally and from around the world, share property, offer comfort, and push past usual limits of fatigue and strength, risking their own lives to help those in need. We call the response "heroic" in order to cover our shame for past failures to help. We know the response is no more and no less than a normal human reaction. We struggle with the uncomfortable knowledge that awareness of human interdependence and the exercise of compassion are simply necessary to the survival of any human community, yet we have been guilty of ignoring both.

We have grown accustomed to the failure of the contemporary family to meet the needs of its individual members. We are no longer shocked when a blood relative is unwilling or unable to care for a family member. Increasingly, it is the larger community, the state, that is expected to carry the ultimate responsibility to care for individuals in need. There is nothing inherently good or bad about this change. It is an integral part of a larger change in our understanding of social responsibility and community.

We are surprised, however, when we see individuals who carry neither the traditional responsibility of "blood relatives" nor the newer responsibility of "state" deplete their own resources in order to care for someone in need. Like the people involved in the "heroic" response to natural disaster, these caring people stir our pride and shame.

We take particular notice if a person dares to step outside the boundaries of traditional sex roles to offer caring. We take special notice of the single man who adopts a physically handicapped baby or the woman who initiates clandestine, dangerous meetings with a group of terrorists in the hope of negotiating release of hostages.

In societies like ours, women have been trained since childhood to offer nurturing care. They are expected to be responsible for cooking, cleaning, and making the home comfortable; to feed, clothe, bathe, instruct, and comfort the young children; and to care for the sick and comfort the distressed. Men are trained from childhood to be responsible for the welfare and safety of all, carrying the financial responsibility of the provider and aggressively protecting the women and children. Of course, individuals vary considerably in their ability and willingness to fulfill such sexual sterotypes. Some women are not, by nature, nurturing. Some men are not, by nature, aggressive. Of those who are, many are no longer willing to stay within the boundaries of the stereotypes.

As more and more women move away from caretaking and nurturing roles, there is a corresponding, but as yet insufficient, movement of men to fill the void. Newspapers and magazines show our interest in nurturing fathers, "house husbands," and dual-career couples who split the responsibilities of homemaking and child care. We are becoming increasingly comfortable with seeing women in jobs that were traditionally reserved for men, but we are more slow and less comfortable in accepting men in jobs traditionally reserved for women. It is the silent shadow of homophobia in our culture that causes the discomfort.

A man in the rare traditional woman's role, such as the spouse of an elected government official, is an acceptable novelty. This is true also for the woman in the rare traditional man's position that is a nurturing role, such as the physician. The greatest discomfort is experienced when men are found in traditional nurturing roles. For this reason, there has been a more swift movement of women into the traditional male-nurturing jobs than there has been of men into the traditional female-nurturing jobs. A female physician is more easily accepted than a male nurse.

Women who step out into what was once the world of men can be more readily understood. They are gaining power and prestige. They are demonstrating that they can be aggressive and competitive. We value these traits in our society.

Men who step into what was once the world of women are less easily understood. They lose male power and prestige. Rather than demonstrating their ability to be aggressive and competitive, they are demonstrating their ability to be caring or nurturing. We do not value this ability as highly. There is a not-so-secret suspicion that such men are not fully men. Therefore, reads the script of homophobia, they are probably gay.

That is an incorrect line of reasoning but it is often rewarded by a correct conclusion. The reasoning that these men wanting to do nurturing "women's work" must not be real men, but female-identified persons who are therefore less than full men, is not correct. The simple reality is that these are men who are more nurture-oriented as individuals, and the increasingly flexible world now permits them to do work appropriate to their interests. Yet, the fact is that a disproportionate number of them *are* gay, so the wrongly reached conclusion is correct.

Less noticeable, but also disturbing to the average citizen, are the women in traditionally male-nurturing positions that do not have any obvious reward in power or prestige. These are the women who are not homemakers but home-builders: the carpenters, plumbers, electricians and roofers. They are also the ranchers, morticians, and airplane mechanics. Again the right conclusion is often reached by the wrong line of reasoning. These are not necessarily women who wish they were men, but women whose natural caretaking interests and abilities carry them more readily into these jobs than into more traditional women's jobs. Yet a disproportionate number of these women *are* lesbians. But, once societal job expectations based on sex role became more flexible, why did these women not rush to other, more powerful and prestigious "male" jobs? Why are they in the "male" caretaking jobs?

Why is there a disproportionate number of gay men in the nurturing positions that society once reserved for women? Why is there a disproportionate number of women in caretaking positions that society once reserved for men? The answer is to be found in the likelihood that a gay man or lesbian is more fully developed in his or her caretaking potential. This phenomenon is assured by the psychodynamics set in motion with the awareness of one's forbidden lovemaking needs.

Not all gay people experience this psychodynamic phenomenon, and not everyone who experiences it is gay, but it is a very common story in the lives of gay people and does help to explain why so many of us have developed our caretaking abilities.

It begins with a dim perception of being unwanted. One person may have been adopted as a newborn infant, and told a

standard story of being "selected" by the adoptive parents. Never-
theless there is a lingering concern as to "why my first parents
didn't want me." Stories of the early death of birth parents do little
to allay the young child's silent assumption that "if they wanted
me, I'd be with them right now."

Another may have been born the seventh child in a family already too poor to feed and shelter themselves. There may be moments of generous love but the very young child senses the anxiety
created by his presence and feels unneeded and unwanted.

Another may have been born into an affluent family just as
the husband and wife were seriously considering divorce. The
very young child is an inconvenience, a representation of the parents' ambivalent conflict. The very young child senses the discomfort when people look at her, and feels unwanted.

There are dozens of variations on this theme. Many children
are simultaneously wanted and unwanted. Ambivalent parents,
siblings, and other family members are apt to try to hide their
guilty half-wish that the new child did not exist. But the infant,
whose life depends upon the ability to sense safety and well-being,
is alerted by subtle signals that life is not secure.

Though the scientific investigation is not yet considered complete, it is reasonable to assume that there is a biological foundation for gender preference similar to the genetic codes that determine the color of hair and eyes or the preference for left hand or
right. Our world produces more people who have dark hair, dark
eyes, are right-handed, and have heterosexual preference; but
there are plenty of us who have light hair, see through blue, green
or gray eyes, are left-handed, or have a sexual preference for
people of the same gender.

There was a time, not long ago, when children who showed
left-hand preference were trained to use their right hand. Such is
the strength of conformity in a society. The assumption was that
since most people were born with right-hand preference, it would
be best for the child to learn to "fit in" and be able to enjoy the easy
use of right-handed tools and customs. Today we realize that such
training was emotionally and physically costly to those naturally
left-handed children. Even so, early signs of left-hand preference

can cause anxiety to right-handed parents today. It is not difficult for young children to sense that life would be easier and perhaps safer if they were different. The exact nature of the difference may be unclear, especially if the parent has been educated in child development. But there exists that primitive sense of danger for the child. The parental lack of ease, however mild, communicates an unsafe environment to the young child.

So it is for the child whose hand use preference is "different" or "wrong," and so it is for the child whose sexual orientation is "different" and therefore "wrong." The child usually senses the danger that comes with being "different" and "unwanted" before the parent realizes it.

A man of twenty-nine told me that when he went home for the Christmas holidays the family had "an orgy of family films." He was not as enthusiastic as other family members when the film showing began. "I didn't think about it really, I just felt reluctant. You know, why go back into all that past? Let's live in the here and now. And my brother and sister were so weirdly enthusiastic. Well, after the third reel, they were getting bored and I was getting interested."

What he saw after the third reel reminded him of the dim, uncomfortable feelings of early childhood that he had mentally suppressed. "There was a big dinner with the relatives all dressed up. I must have been about three years old and they were trying to keep me occupied. My mother put me in the lap of my aunt who tried to entertain me with hugs, kisses and funny faces. I squirmed off her lap, disappeared under the table and appeared in the lap of my uncle across the table. My mother took me, held me for a few seconds, and gave me back to my aunt. Under the table I went and appeared again in the arms of my uncle. It repeated three times and each time my mother's face looked more strained. I think it would be fair to say she looked angry. I thought at first it might be because I was thwarting her control, always a problem for Mom, but I saw the same look on her face in the next reel when I put my arms around my six-year-old brother and gave him a sloppy kiss on the mouth."

He said he could remember how much he wanted to be in

touch with his uncle and his older brother and, at the same time, he remembered an uncomfortable feeling. "But my hair stood on end as we watched that scene of me smooching my brother and my mother laughed and said, "You were always such a sweet kid but sometimes I could have killed you — always bothering somebody." There it was. The evidence was on the screen and out of my mom's mouth. My uncle hadn't looked bothered, nor had my brother. They were both enjoying it. But my mother didn't like it one little bit."

A woman who told me similar tales of early childhood said, "My girlfriend and I used to take turns pretending we were mother and baby, you know, holding one another, singing some crazy lullaby, or feeding one another with a nursing bottle filled with water. It drove my whole family crazy. They used to hide the bottle and fix me up with little boys from three blocks away. My father once told me it was dangerous to feed one another the bottle that way because we might choke one another!"

Whether or not there are other identifiable factors early in the life of the gay child that set the stage for feeling unwanted and "wrong," the first signs of same-gender attraction have a result similar to, but stronger than the first appearance of left-hand preference. The parents are made uncomfortable by non-conforming difference. The child senses the discomfort and becomes wary in an environment that seems unsafe. It is a natural, animal response; in the wilderness, a parent animal's discomfort alerts the young to possible danger.

Just as the young animal in the wild quickly learns to "read" the tension or discomfort of the adult and become more alert to the sights, smells, and sounds of the surroundings, so does the young human become alert and wary. The more uncomfortable the child's difference makes the surrounding people, the more alert and wary the child is apt to be.

A positive result of this phenomenon is that the child is likely to develop heightened sensitivity. Such a child, feeling less secure, is more devoted to learning to "read" the cues of the environment. Nonverbal, unconscious emotions are noticed as they are transmitted in posture, tone of voice, subtle facial cues of pleasure or tension, and seemingly random selection of particular words or topics of conversation, particularly if the nonverbal, nonconscious communication is in direct opposition to the spoken communication. And, just as other young animals, unsure of their safety, become alert to all aspects of their environment — sounds, colors, movement, odors, and any disruption of the natural background harmony — so is this sensitivity heightened for the "different" child. It may explain the often noticed correlation of "feeling different" and "aesthetic awareness" in the young. The heightened sensitivity is developed for survival.

The young human who develops this heightened sensitivity, including the ability to "read" people's nonverbal emotional communication, learns to conform in outward appearance as much as possible because it makes other people more comfortable and eases the sense of unsafety in the environment. But such a child is often noticed because of his more fully developed compassion.

One woman told me, "By the time I was nine years old I was consciously trying to fit in. I didn't want to be a faint-hearted cry-baby like the girl next door. Her little-lady swoons and dramas looked pretty phony to me anyway. But I sure noticed when the teacher looked depressed or angry. I noticed when the boy with the stutter looked scared at recess, so I tried to befriend him. And I noticed my father's feelings covered over with concrete when he shot a bird or a squirrel for sport."

On the street recently, I saw an exasperated woman slap her young daughter full across the face and saw the girl's younger brother burst into tears. Compassion means to "feel with," and that is what he did.

In the complex chain of learned survival skills, the developing young gay person may learn to mask his more highly developed compassion but it is apt to be present. The mother of a gay man once told me, "He was always so tender-hearted." I have heard similar statements from relatives many times. Her tone of voice indicated that she still did not know what to make of this trait in her son. It must have sometimes seemed a virtue and sometimes an embarrassment or a nuisance. But always, it had captured her attention as something odd about her son. He was, in her words, "tender-hearted"; some would say "soft." It is compassion, a developed involuntary ability to feel the emotions that others are experiencing.

All of us will do anything required to find reasonable safety. Many of us, wary and unsure that we are wanted, seek shelter in the social safety of being needed. It is seldom a conscious process. An often-used phrase is, "I just feel better if I'm *doing* something." That something is, more often than not, designed to make the world a better place for someone else. Such behavior alters the internalized judgement of "unwanted." Instead one feels "useful." If a person's self-esteem has been damaged, first by feeling unwanted, then learning to feel bad, wrong, or sinful for hidden gay feelings, "useful" behavior is a desperately needed tonic. If one can feel a bit more wanted, a bit less wrong or bad, it is possible to feel a bit more safe in an unsafe world. People are less likely to harm you if they need you. Useful behavior becomes as necessary a part of life as any drug to which people can become addicted. Many of us are noticed in our caretaking because our helping behavior has reached the stage of a helping addiction.

A weary man in his mid-twenties appeared in my office several years ago. He was depressed, having trouble sleeping, and was plagued with bouts of unexpected, unexplained crying. "I've tried to just get on with the things I have to do. It's always worked before, but I'm having trouble concentrating at work." He was a nurse who had been "acting night supervisor" at his hospital for two years. He was supporting his lover, who was working on an M.B.A. degree. He was also sending money home to his widowed, ailing mother who lived two thousand miles away. His former lover had been involved in a serious automobile accident and was staying with him while he recuperated. And there was a strong possibility that his former lover also had a drug dependency and was dealing drugs. "I've been asking for several months when I'll be promoted from 'acting' to night supervisor; the increase of pay would help a lot. But the administrator is caught in a bind. There just isn't enough money and we're understaffed as it is."

When I saw him the next week, he had had no sleep for more than twenty-four hours. "I had to bail out the next-door neighbor's wife, who has a drinking problem and was picked up for drunk driving. They're divorced, but he was out of town on business and the kids were home alone."

This man had become a helping addict. When I gently pointed out that he was doing more than could reasonably be expected of one person, he smiled and looked relieved. "That's what comes of growing up in a big family, I guess," he said. "I've always had to do what I can."

A month later he said, "I guess I just need to be needed." Six months later he said, "I think maybe I'm doing too much but I don't know how to change it." That, of course, was the real beginning of his recuperation. He had caught a glimpse of his addiction.

During the peak of the recent wave of sexual liberation, some people found themselves carried far beyond the relief of freedom. These people, especially if they were considered quite attractive by current standards, found that they were wanted and "needed" by many people — at least for purposes of sexual intercourse. Frequent sexual activity distracted them from other concerns and became the opiate necessary for maintenance of comfort by a person addicted to helping.

With the advent of the AIDS epidemic, and the realization that it was probably a sexually transmitted disease, the wave of sexual liberation sweeping the Western world radically and suddenly changed in the gay community. At about that time a male couple consulted me. They had been together in a satisfying relationship for fifteen years. For six of those years it had been an open relationship that included other sexual partners. With the recognition of the AIDS epidemic they had decided to return to a monogamous relationship. The problem came when they discovered that one of them was unable to do so. At first it seemed that it was a matter of their life having changed and one of them simply being unwilling to return to monogamy.

"We've worked out our own problems together over the years and we trust one another," the non-addicted man said. "So Joe and I tried a few experiments that included other men for safe sex. It wasn't working. And then we decided to give monogamy a wholehearted try for six months..."

"It was a disaster," Joe said. "I had to admit that something was way out of control for me. I felt real anxious and scared. I had nightmares. One night I manipulated Paul into taking a sleeping pill and as soon as he was sound asleep I was dressed and out the door headed for some fast sex. That was it. I remembered a friend of ours doing the same thing to get out and get some booze because he's an alcoholic. So when Paul woke up in the morning I just broke down and said, 'I've got a problem and I can't fix it.' And I've been fixing other people's problems all my life." The man addicted to helping had become addicted to "helping" with sex. His constant sexual activity with a wide variety of partners seemed to offer a reassurance that he was wanted, needed, and therefore, oddly, more safe in the world.

A woman in her mid-forties consulted me when she and her gay husband were approaching a divorce. She had reached the threshold of a new level of clarity. She said, "I think there is hope for my sanity because I finally see how crazy I am. I have been seriously involved with three alcoholics, including my recently sober father who's now in A.A., and four women dependent on drugs. I got crazy trying to fix things I couldn't fix. I needed to do the impossible so that I'd be allowed a place in this world. I've always known I'm a lesbian. So what do I do for one last try? I seduce a gay man into marriage and convince myself that we'll become heterosexuals. And I was crazy enough to think it was all the people I was trying to help who had the problems. Well, I'm here for me, not them. God bless, and I hope they find their way, but it's about time I looked at the mess I'm making of my own life."

Certainly, most gay people do not become helping addicts. It does not become that extreme. But the underlying dynamics are the same. The gay person is apt to feel unwanted and "bad" or "wrong" early in life. He discovers that he feels better when contributing to a better world in some way. In so doing one feels needed. And it feels safer to feel needed.

We develop caretaking talents that make it easy for people to depend upon us as doctor, lawyer, house-builder, decorator, hairdresser, gardener, entertainer, teacher, confidante or legislator. Less visible to the non-gay world, we are often impressed when we glimpse the extent of our collective responsibility for the well-being of the established social structure. We are, very often, the people others turn to when they are in need.

How and why does this tending, nurturing, or caring capacity develop so strongly in some people? Why does it seem to be so strikingly present in the community of gay people? The development of this caretaking potential is adaptive for the gay person. It helps to assure our survival in a threatening environment. We have used our natural talents and potential for caretaking and developed them as if our lives depended on it.

Caring for Life Together

Supermarket lines have their utility, as do most of the unpleasant by-products of changing contemporary life. They offer an opportunity not only to see what people are eating but also to hear what people are thinking. I recently found myself in a long line, behind two high-school students who were discussing their assignment: to write a paper about simple sex roles and the basic values of society.

The young woman, who was chewing bubble gum and plaiting a modest strand from a vast supply of hair, said, "Look, it's always the women who have to take care of the kids — at least in the beginning. I mean, you guys still can't get pregnant so women start off taking care of everybody in the beginning of their lives."

Her companion was a tall, thin young man with very little hair. He toyed pensively with his one earring. "Yeah, but the men usually have to do the protecting. I mean, like you can't take care of the kids if the town isn't safe."

She popped her bubble with a snap and pointed her finger in his direction. "Okay, so you guys are out dropping bombs to keep us safe but we still have to get pregnant, give birth, feed the kids, take care of them when they're sick, put them in clothes, clean up after them, and teach them to walk and talk. You can do all the protecting you want but there's no life to protect unless we produce babies and take care of them."

I wondered how they would react if I asked what they thought of the role of gay people in the caretaking of young and old. But I knew the long line was not long enough to add still another level of complexity to their discussion.

It seems evident that women carry the primary responsibility for caretaking in most societies, just as it seems clear that protection is a competitive business. If our planet is seen as one community that contains smaller communities, then damaging and destroying life on the planet in order to protect it must be seen as foolish. Making more efficient weapons of destruction while people starve is not a sane way to improve the quality of human life.

Of course, some women are poorly suited for caretaking and some men are able to fill caretaking roles very well. It is quite acceptable for men to build homes, become healers and teachers, and try to negotiate peace. In rapidly changing contemporary societies, some manage to feed, tend, and teach the very young also, just as some women are now permitted to enter male caretaking positions.

Lesbians and gay men are a large minority but are a minority still, estimated to be between ten and fifteen percent of the population. Certainly we are not responsible for all of the caretaking. But we are disproportionately well represented in caretaking roles because of our survival-oriented need to be needed. Because we have crossed the artificial barrier of culturally prescribed sex roles, we are apt to bring the ease of a male/female balanced orientation to caretaking tasks, thereby making more conventional people uneasy.

A young lesbian told me how suspicious the graduate school admissions committee was because she had taken two years after her undergraduate studies to work as a policewoman. She came from a privileged background. She knew that police work would give her a broader view of human behavior, feelings and attitudes. It reminded me of my own experience with an undergraduate psychology advisor, who was uneasy about me, first for wanting to take art and literature courses, and then for wanting to work as an assistant kindergarten teacher. People are intrigued but somewhat uncomfortable if a young man wants to teach kindergarten, just as they are about a young woman wanting to work as a uniformed police officer. Had I chosen the police work and she the kindergarten work, it would have been more easily accepted by our elders — and we would not have learned as much. I needed to learn more from the point of view of the traditional female caretaker and she needed to learn more from the point of view of the traditional male caretaker. We sensed it would give us greater strength and balance, and we were not frightened to step out of the traditional sex roles.

While anyone may fall into the trap of the helping addict, it is more of a risk for the gay man or the lesbian. The non-gay woman in a typical caretaking role of wife and mother may be subject to problems of low self-esteem that were seeded by special circumstances and events early in life. The non-gay man in a typical caretaking role of "breadwinner" for a large family may be subject to similar problems. To stave off the anxiety that comes with too-easily perceived feelings of inadequacy, the woman may become a Super Mom who minds everyone's business and gives more help than anyone wants. The man may become Super Dad and overcome fantastic odds to give his wife and children advantages that rob them of the opportunity to develop their own initiative. For the average non-gay woman or man, the urge to go to such extremes does not exist. For the average gay man or lesbian there is, however, a natural incentive — the wish to find safety by being needed in a world that constantly tells us we are unwanted.

Being needed, and thereby seemingly assured of safety, does not sufficiently provide the basic sense of well-being we all seek in life. Experience repeatedly teaches us that the needs of today are not the needs of tomorrow. Security comes from an enduring feeling of belonging or being wanted. To feel secure, you need the assurance that you are valued, not because of what you can do for others, but because you are an asset as you are.

Trying to find one's way in this world as a gay person with well-developed caretaking abilities, it is very easy to reach repeatedly for the seeming safety of being needed. But most needs we satisfy are no more than transient debris in a sea of constant change. The needs are temporary and not sturdy enough to keep us afloat. And so we are tempted to reach out to the next need and the next, becoming addicted to being needed, attaching ourselves to needy people and helping them to remain needy as we tend their needs.

This is a more striking phenomenon in the gay community than in the larger community. It is easy for a gay person to become dependent on being needed. When the dependency has become an addiction, she is more apt to be noticed within the gay community, where we are familiar with the lure and the danger of this opiate. It is harder to con a con; and an over-compensating need addict is easily recognized by a person who is one or is recovering from the addiction. It is our willingness to recognize the presence and danger of this opiate in our communty that has kept it within reasonable control. We are, after all, a community heavily endowed with caretaking talents and abilities. Odd as it might seem in the larger world, it is natural for us to offer help, not only to a person who appears needy, but also to the person who is addicted to offering help.

Caring help is most effective when it is no more than a gentle offering, available when wanted. Sometimes the addicted person finds the needed help in the process of psychotherapy, after friends have helped by refusing to feed the addiction.

One man told me, "I feel scared. I don't know what I'm doing wrong. My friends don't seem to have much use for me anymore. I'm busy as hell at work, not only doing the job but also helping everybody and their cousin put out fires in their personal lives. I'm giving more than I should in volunteer work. Then I come home alone and exhausted and that's all there is — I'm just alone and exhausted. Something's wrong. I can't go on this way much longer."

He remembered a time when friends would call about a domestic dispute, or would ask him to come for dinner and then pour out their troubles about work to him, or how often he would organize a surprise party or a fundraising benefit. "No one seems to care about anything, now. They don't call anymore. Everyone seems busy with their own lives. I miss the old times and the sharing."

It took him time to see that he missed the feeling of being needed for help. A turning point came when an old friend he had not seen for several years telephoned unexpectedly. "I was surprised to hear his voice but I recognized it right away. I said, 'What's the matter?' There was a second of silence and then we both laughed. I mean, that's how it used to be. Whenever he called, something was the matter and I needed to find out right away so I could help. When he started to grow up and not need so much help from me, we drifted apart. There has to be more to a friendship than that!"

But letting go can be frightening. Finding people who seem to need your help and facilitating the continuation of their need yields a very temporary sense of security. You have a hold on those people. Their need is a justification for your existence. Loosening your hold, letting go of them, is frightening because it seems likely that they will drift away, gravitating to other people who can help them, leaving you alone and without a justification for living.

When you loosen your hold and let go, the chronically needy drift away, possibly forever, at least until they become able to satisfy their own needs. No matter how much reassurance the helping addict is given, ultimately she must trust the care and help being offered by non-addicted caretakers, especially those who once were as addicted to helping. It is necessary to lean on these recovering people temporarily while converting the energy that once went to patching up other people's lives into energy now used in building one's own satisfying life.

The man described earlier referred to this letting go as "the most scary and exciting experience I've ever had. Every day I wake up with a moment of panic and then I remember that it's *my* life that is getting better now. I am beginning to have friends who like me because they like *me*. I don't have to knock them over with my help. And every day my life just gets better as I tend to my own business and respect other people's right to go about their business their own way. I had the world's greatest collection of crutches — all the people who couldn't get along without my help. It still feels funny not having all those crutches in my arms but my hands are free and my arms are opening." He had learned how to use his well-developed caretaking abilities without becoming dependent on them.

Often, a person with highly developed caretaking abilities is fond of plants and animals. This man was an avid gardener. Two years after I first met him he said, "You know, my garden has changed completely. It used to be full of plants that don't do well in this part of the world. I moved things indoors and then out, controlled the temperature and the amount of light, rearranged the chemical and mineral content of the soil and the entire garden was dependent upon my wonderful efforts. Now the garden is full of plants that grow naturally in this area. I still tend them. I water, prune and spray, but it's not such a constant occupation. The garden wouldn't be as beautiful without my efforts, but all the plants in it could get along without me." He was helping them to find life, not finding and forcing plants that would be dependent on his care. He had gotten free of his helping addiction and was experiencing the rewards of caretaking.

We gay men and lesbians have done far more than our share of tending the needs of the young by feeding, clothing, comforting and educating. We have also done far more than our share of healing, nursing and tending the needs of the adult community with building, gardening, negotiating, teaching, guiding, counseling, entertaining, cleaning up and beautifying the environment. We have had to develop our potential in these areas as best we could because our well-being has seemed to depend on it.

Human behavior that was adaptive thousands of years ago is maladaptive now. Suppression of "masculine" talents in women and "feminine" talents in men is now counterproductive to the well-being of the human community. We can afford to, and need

to, develop all talents that enrich life. The competitive, aggressive
stance traditionally considered "masculine" is very costly to the
human community. It is an excellent example of rigid tradition in
a conformity-oriented society. People become the conforming victims of such counterproductive traditions.

All life is involved in constant change. A society that is
unable to change because its conformity orientation makes it too
obedient to tradition is destined to crumble. A building or a tree
that cannot yield to the demands of wind or shifting earth must
fall. It is flexibility that permits adaption to change.

But most of our societies are conformity-oriented. We obey
community rules or laws so that people can live together. When
law-abiding behavior becomes habitual, the community offers
reasonable safety to its individual members. Yet, if there is a progressive intensification of devotion to the rules, the society becomes too rigid and unyielding to change. Something must inter-
fere, forcing re-examination and reinterpretation of existing rules
to meet the changing times.

One persistent non-conforming force in every human society
does not attack life or property, and thus poses no threat to safety.
It is homoeroticism. But just as societies become conformity-
oriented to insure the following of community rules, they also encourage heterosexual behavior to assure the production of future
generations. Heterosexuality thereby becomes an unquestioned
part of conformity in communities. Yet, conformity-oriented,
heterosexual-encouraging societies continue to produce people
with homosexual inclinations as regularly as they produce people
who are left-handed.

To the narrow-minded, this seems to be both a puzzle and a
problem, and thus many elaborate explanations are often based
on superstition and prejudice. But all scientific evidence suggests
that homoerotic inclination is as natural as heteroerotic. Both fall
on a continuum of natural attraction-potential that ranges from
very strong to very weak for different individuals. Circumstances
will, of course, influence the development of the potential as it
takes form in the first few years of life. Those people with the

strongest homoerotic potential will resist the prevalent hetero-sexual orientation of the community and continue into adult life with conscious awareness of homoerotic preference. Such people appear in all places and times with the same regularity as left-handed people in right-handed communities. Depending on the relative strength of both the homoerotic and heteroerotic poten-tial, some people will appear to have no particular preference, just as some people appear to be ambidextrous. Of course, in a society that strongly encourages both heteroerotic interest and right-handedness, people must have a somewhat strong potential for homoeroticism or left-handedness in order to overcome the dis-couragement experienced in early training. In a society more tol-erant of natural preferences, one sees more homoerotic interest and more left-handedness. It is that simple.

While left-handedness was an emotional issue that seemed more threatening to the conforming society in the last century, it has become fairly well accepted today as the natural human varia-tion it is. Homoerotic preference continues to frighten people, however. While the individuals with the strongest homoerotic preference, gay men and lesbians, have suffered much abuse as a result, the phenomenon has helped heteroerotic-conforming soci-eties to survive in a world of accelerating social change.

Everyone is related by family, occupation and/or friendship to people who are gay. It may be that open recognition of the les-bian or gay man has not been permitted, and perhaps the words have not been spoken aloud, but the connection exists. Some gay people are more visible than others. But ten to fifteen percent of the population, regardless of family social class, ethnic group, or nationality, have a homoerotic preference strong enough to qual-ify them as gay. It would be a rare, isolated person who could avoid contact with any of us.

By our very numbers we have helped to keep contemporary societies sufficiently flexible. No matter how repressive the social environment and how willing the individual citizen is to embrace absolute fundamental conformity, that person often must come to terms with the inner knowledge that a daughter, son, aunt, uncle, cousin, parent, friend, or colleague is one of "them" — a good person who is an innocent outlaw.

I spent many hours with a married couple who lived in an extremely repressive community. They were suffering terrible guilt. They had known for years that their son was gay, and they had approved his move from their small town to a large city a thousand miles away, supposedly for purposes of career advancement. They had never admitted the true reason to one another. They also were aware that the man's uncle and the woman's sister were "that way," but they never discussed it. When the man's cousin was arrested, tried, convicted and sent to prison because he was enticed and entrapped by a "vice officer" in the next county, they remained silent. When a friend, who was also the pastor of their church, had to leave the area because of rampant suspicion that his erotic interests were "deviant," they accepted it.

It was not until their beloved grandchild was severely beaten, disfigured, and had to go to a boarding school to ensure his safety, that their conforming defenses crumbled. The boy was the son of their admired eldest daughter and her husband, who was the high school football coach. None of his schoolmates had been suspicious of him. His same-gender attraction was confirmed when he followed a particularly attractive classmate into a dark classroom on the evening of the seventh grade dance. The others were in hiding there, ready to pounce when the boy leaned forward for the invited embrace. The man was a person of few words. On our first meeting, his wife sobbed as he soberly shook his head and repeatedly said, "It isn't right. He did no harm. It isn't right."

All societies demand some degree of conformity, yet must have that conformity challenged so that rules remain open to question and change. Societies encourage heterosexuality but they profit from the challenge of undeniable homoerotic preference within all segments of the population. Willing or not, we gay men and lesbians serve this important caretaking function in our communities. We cannot be explained away, nor has it ever been possible to deny awareness of our existence for very long.

A government may deny our presence but we are there. A community may put us in prisons or hospitals, try to change us with psychotherapy or torture, exile us in relocation or quarantine programs, but they continue to give birth to us as their daughters and sons. They may not realize that we are serving a caretaking function for them, merely by our persistent existence. Nonetheless, they must contend with our being part of them. In confronting them with their inhumane treatment of us, we confront them with the folly of their blind conformity and their rigid adherence to the rules. The rules must be questioned and made changeable, lest people continue to sacrifice their own offspring and perpetuate a society whose rigid rules will ultimately destroy everyone.

Of course, we serve another vital caretaking function for the entire community. We are the males who dare to see, hear, and understand with our "feminine" abilities also; the women who dare to see, hear, and understand with our undenied "masculine" abilities. Thus, we have served as the "seers" always. We are the people able to see in depth because we use both eyes, hear in depth because we use both ears, understand in depth because we use that which has been reserved for male understanding and also that which has been reserved for female understanding. We can be both nurturing and protective, yielding and assertive. Less hidden in the past, respected as seers, oracles, and counselors, we continue in contemporary costumes to serve as advisors and negotiators, and people sometimes described as having an uncanny ability to anticipate future change. The "uncanny ability" of today was the same ability that created martyrs and fueled witch hunts in the past. People who have accepted the sex-role repression of their society are made uneasy by people who are not similarly repressed. The more repressive the society, the greater the collective anxiety and the greater the likelihood that those least capable of enlightened leadership will galvanize the collective anxiety in the population and initiate a purge of "those people."

Times of purge are dangerous for everyone. In the wave of hysteria that accompanies the purge, many quite ordinary people are accused of being "one of them" and, consequently, persecuted. The greatest danger, of course, in addition to the obvious injustice, is that the society will discover and destroy too many of us, leaving it impoverished of the ability to anticipate change and create adequate adaptation. The danger lies in the destruction of too many of a society's caretakers.

I talked with a man who had been a boy in two Nazi concentration camps. He witnessed an eerie event. In the final months of that social disaster, several high-ranking German officers came to the camp to consult some of the gypsies and two homosexuals who wore the pink triangle. It was clear that the end of the current German rule was near and they sought advice and personal counsel about the future. Both the gypsies and the men with the pink triangles told them they had no advice to offer. It was clear to them that these men were destined to live with their awesome guilt in the final days of a society that had committed suicide by its worship of conformity and by separating itself from its seers.

The potential for such purges continues, and their possible consequences are increasingly dangerous. As the contemporary world becomes more efficient in its invasion of privacy and its ability to identify individual differences without respecting them, it becomes more and more likely that the gay person will be discovered, whether willing to make the disclosure or not.

A purge in the near future could destroy so many caretakers that the future of all humans would be at risk. It is a question that will demand its answer soon. Will gay men and lesbians, with their caretaking difference be appreciated — or will there be an efficient purge that, by putting us in absolute danger, will put all human life at risk? One already can see the movement of gay people in the direction of life-protecting adaptation as more lesbians choose to become mothers with gay male donor fathers, thereby increasing the genetic likelihood of gay children.

In television talk shows and letters to the editor, it is easy today to find the person who "can't understand why they need to flaunt their difference." They do not understand why we are unwilling to continue to pose as something we are not. And some people are concerned that gay men and lesbians have become so assertive in demanding legislative protection of civil rights and have banded together in political action groups or have chosen to live near one another in a new form of urban ghetto.

A lesbian friend of a gay man, who could not speak for himself because he was near death as a result of AIDS, explained it to several of his family members this way: "John and I got this close because we had something in common. I love my family just as he loves you. But my family would not see me as the person I am. I was an embarrassment to them. They wanted me to be someone I am not. I don't think either John or I would have become so political or so vocal except that we needed to be recognized as the good people we are, entitled to the same rights as other people. Once you can see us, love us, and appreciate us for the people we are, we will no longer have to be separate. We never wanted to be separate. We need you and love you. And you need us."

Two Epidemics

When the AIDS epidemic reached gay males, there was concern, but we had experienced more than our fair share of sexually transmitted diseases already. There was no way for us to know in the beginning that this was a lethal epidemic more deadly than any experienced in our lifetimes. As friends developed a bizarre variety of symptoms leading to early death, it seemed to be many diseases rather than one, and how people became infected was not known. Nor was it yet known that the disease already existed elsewhere in the world in a predominantly heterosexual population. Fear was intense when we learned there was no effective treatment and no cure.

But our collective reaction was amazing. With very few exceptions, we did not abandon one another. While fearing for our lives, we did not run from one another. This deadly epidemic revealed our nature as lovemakers and caretakers. We quickly reached out with every resource we had, offering our love and care in every form to those among us who were sick and dying.

Humans have a sorry history of creating rationalizations based on superstition or religion that permit inhumane treatment of the sick and dying. Fear can easily lead to hysteria. Loved ones often are left to their own devices when symptoms of an incurable epidemic disease appear. During the Plague, parents left diseased children on the streets to die alone. Not too many years ago, lepers were thrown from boats into the ocean near the island of Molokai, to sink or swim.

As this unknown disease appeared among gay men in the United States and Europe, it was first labeled "Gay Related Immuno-Deficiency," or GRID, since it was recognized that the immune system of these gay men was for some reason dysfunctional, making them vulnerable to opportunistic diseases that a person with a healthy immune system could fight off. Two diseases began to appear with regularity, KS (Kaposi's Sarcoma), and PCP (Pneumocystis Carinii Pneumonia).

A man in one of my ongoing weekly psychotherapy groups developed an odd variety of symptoms and died before the epidemic was recognized. A month after that, a friend called to tell me that he had received a diagnosis of KS. The following week another friend telephoned and told me he had been admitted to the hospital with a diagnosis of PCP. An era had begun.

When I went to the hospital to visit the friend who was fighting PCP, he was in a very small isolation room. There was a sign on the door advising all who entered that they must wear a mask, gown, and gloves. A half-dozen friends were gathered in the hall, waiting to visit, one or two at a time. The door was ajar. I noticed that, despite our apprehension about this lethal disease that was transmitted from one person to another in an unknown manner, each person who entered the room found some way to make physical contact. We who know the lonely pain of living without the loving physical contact we need were determined to give that contact.

And the afternoon was not without our own brand of brave humor. As one intense, usually reserved, man reached a gloved hand to touch the hand of the man in bed, he said, "Pardon the prophylactic. It's new, you know. The sexual fashion industry has expanded its line to hands this season."

Later, an unreformed drag queen, with the ruthless humor that has carried us through other dangerous times, said, "Really, darling, I love the idea of a hospital theme party but if you had just thought to send out the invitations a wee bit earlier I'm sure we would have been much more inventive with our gloves, masks, and certainly the gowns! And perhaps a tune like the *Lavender Code Blues*. And I thought PCP was a new drug!"

Another man stood in the doorway before entering and said, "Before I cover half my face with this mask, read my lips. I love you." And he kissed the silent air as a tear appeared on his cheek, and mine. Whatever was going to happen, we would not be alone, we would not abandon one another.

A year later, my friend died. By then many others were sick and dying. By then we knew it was a disease caused by a virus that attacks cells that are a vital part of a healthy functioning immune system, and that the virus is transmitted from one person's blood to another's, usually by sexual intercourse, intravenous injection, or blood transfusion. By then we knew that the long-invisible incubation period of the disease had coincided with a unique period of intense sexual interaction among gay men, and therefore many of us had been exposed to the virus and were at risk of developing the disease now known as "Acquired Immune Deficiency Syndrome," or AIDS. Ironically, by then we knew that the virus was nondiscriminatory and, thus, was not a "gay" disease. It was ironic, because by then the bigots were preaching that God had selected AIDS as punishment for gay men.

With their hate-filled propaganda the anti-gay bigots put the non-gay population at risk, deluding them with the false belief that they were safe from the supposedly gay disease. Because of its long, invisible incubation period, AIDS infected many non-gay people during that period. The propagandists then began to change their hate mongering, charging that gay men had given the disease to "innocent" non-gay people.

In the first few years of the AIDS epidemic, public funds were desperately needed for proper medical treatment, education aimed at risk reduction and prevention, and medical research that might lead to appropriate treatment, prevention and cure. Such public funding was scarce and given reluctantly and slowly because the disease appeared to be restricted to an unfavored minority group. It was a lesson costly in lost lives, painful suffering, and money — if, indeed, the lesson has been learned. Perhaps one day we will realize that the suffering of some ultimately causes all to suffer.

Gay men were joined in the early months of the epidemic by lesbians as well as non-gay friends and family members whose love was strong enough to transcend fear. With stunning speed, a variety of privately-funded support services and fundraising events appeared. Educational programs disseminated information that dramatically curbed transmission of the disease and calmed much of the unnecessary fear. In hospitals, doctors, nurses, paraprofessionals and others volunteered to work with AIDS patients. Support programs provided food, housing, and volunteers to cook, clean, counsel, and comfort people with AIDS. Our caretaking was well under way.

Increased pressure was brought to bear on governments to provide needed funding. As we reached out with hands and money to help one another, we began to see our lovemaking and caretaking more clearly. Countless times I heard people describe how deeply satisfying it was to be of help and how gratified they were when their volunteer efforts brought them into loving contact with a gay person whom they might not otherwise have met. We learned quickly, or were reminded, that our attraction to one another goes beyond the superficial differences that seem to be impenetrable barriers in the larger society.

A senior partner in a law firm told me of his attempt to explain to a genuinely baffled colleague why he was not only making generous financial contributions to various AIDS organizations, but was also going each week to clean the home of a man with AIDS who did not have the strength to do it himself.

"But you pay someone to clean your own place," his puzzled colleague said. "Why not send a cleaning service?"

"I told him that, first of all, plenty of professional house cleaners would be afraid of catching something and would go there reluctantly, if at all. When you're sick you don't need that kind of person in your home. And I *like* to go. I help him out into the living room usually and make some tea for both of us. Then, after I vacuum, we talk while I'm doing the more quiet cleaning. We compare experiences from the past. He's just a little younger and we talk about crushes we had, how we came out to various family members, and all the funny and sad things that happened along the way. We've grown really fond of one another. The visits are good for both of us. Sometimes he just naps while I clean. He says it's comforting to hear me moving around the apartment doing things. I know what he means."

Early in the epidemic, before blood banks were able to screen donated blood for evidence of exposure to the virus, the banks refused blood donations from all men who admitted to being gay. Even without the ban, gay men had stopped donating because it seemed likely that blood from an infected person might transmit the disease agent. At the same time, however, blood was needed for transfusions for some of the people with AIDS.

Lesbians formed Blood Sister donation groups. One young lesbian said it simply: "I'm still not happy with male oppression of women in this society," she told me, "but these guys are my brothers. It's a matter of life and death. They'd do the same for me. I work as a volunteer on the AIDS Information Hotline too, and some of the guys who volunteer there have AIDS. I think lesbians and gay men are closer now. I know some guys are staying alive with my lesbian blood and that makes me feel good. Let's face it, some women and kids have the disease already, and more will. When a person needs help or can give it, you're a human being and nothing more."

The outpouring of care, help, and love within the gay community and from our friends in the earliest months and years of the epidemic was a moving testimony of the unselfish generosity that exists in some people. The reluctance of government to act responsibly and the outpouring of hatred from an ugly minority of the population were equally strong reminders of the potential for meanness that also resides in the human community.

Jobs were lost, families torn apart, and people were to die without the comfort of family, familiar surroundings, or their religion because fear and hatred found the opportunity to bond. Those who believe they have the right to speak for God took to the task quickly and righteously, as they have done for thousands of years. The suffering caused as a direct result of their pseudo-pious inhumanity is immense. I talked with one young man who had been sent from church and family in Salt Lake City with one hundred dollars and the assurance that he had sinned beyond redemption. By the time he found his way to safety and shelter in San Francisco, he was only weeks away from death. He was weak with several physical diseases and disoriented with the grief of loss. One of his last coherent statements was, "Tell them that I don't understand." He was speaking of his family and the people back home who said they loved him. "I still love them," he said. And it was he who was supposed by them to have sinned.

One of his sisters tried to be forgiving in a note that arrived the day he died. "I know you didn't mean to do wrong," she said. "You got in with that group of homosexuals and they turned you into one of them. They are like vampires that prey on the innocent. Their sexual appetite can never be satisfied and now it is killing people like you. I am praying for you..."

There were two epidemics under way by then, each as dangerous and costly as the other. One was a disease of the body caused by a virus. The other was a disease of the mind and spirit caused by unchallenged fear, ignorance, superstition and prejudice. The first epidemic was new, the other quite old, and no cure was in sight for either though it could be hoped that education might retard the spread of both.

When it was discovered that AIDS was caused by a virus in the bloodstream, it was clear that the spread of the disease could be slowed by screening blood used for transfusion, attempting to reach, warn, and educate people who shared intravenous needles, and educating people about the potential risks in certain forms of sexual intercourse.

Of the three tasks, the first was the easiest. Tests were developed that detected the presence of antibodies produced by the body to combat the virus, thereby indicating exposure to the virus. Whether such a person was infected and incubating the virus could not be established with certainty by these tests. But the absence of any trace of antibodies did indicate that the virus had not been introduced into the person's blood and the blood was therefore safe for use in transfusions.

Reaching people who shared intravenous needles was a much less hopeful task. Many were people addicted to illegal drugs. Addiction creates an urgency, so that when the drug becomes available, the addict will throw caution to the wind and risk dangerous infection in order to obtain relief. Also, once under the influence of the drug, judgment is likely to be impaired and a person who is ordinarily sensible may take an unnecessary risk.

By far the most difficult task anticipated was the attempt to persuade people to alter habitual sexual practices. One's sense of value, self-esteem, and place in a social hierarchy are all involved in the manner in which each of us has learned to participate in social-sexual rituals. Add to that the fact that orgasm is a mighty reward in learned human behavior, and one can anticipate the dim chances of altering any habitual sexual behavior.

Death from sexually transmitted disease is not new. Before the discovery and use of antibiotics less than fifty years ago, syphilis and gonorrhea were common causes of human misery and death. Education had done little to limit the damage done by these previous diseases. Scare tactics and fear of painful disease and death had proved no match for the (imagined and real) rewards of sexual intercourse.

But, in the case of the AIDS epidemic, within the gay community there were inherent assets that would help in the seemingly hopeless task of quickly altering sexual behavior and slowing the progress of the epidemic. The most basic of these assets is our natural orientation as caretakers.

Gay men were among the active participants in the wave of sexual liberation that swept the Western world, partly because we had been taught that it was sexual appetite that defined us and made us different from other people. But there was another reason. We were trained as men. As part of that training it was expected that we would attempt as many sexually desirable contacts as possible. Also as part of that training it was expected that we would compete with other men to the point of combat. But since the people we found sexually desirable often were other men, there was a conflict.

We could, and did, enjoy multiple sexual contacts. We could, and did, compete for the favor of other sexually attractive males. But the competition had to take a different course from that which would lead to combat. We sought love and caring in our sexual contacts.

The vulnerability that accompanies orgasm, when one is without defense, was a strongly reinforcing pledge of non-combat. We could competitively seek one another's favor but we could not competitively risk destroying one another. To do so would be to risk the loss of the prizes in the competition. It would mean risking the loss of those desired people who might love and care for us. We were obliged to learn to compete, yet also to care, for one another.

As active participants in the wave of sexual freedom, we had learned to use sexual contact with other men as a means of reinforcing our social bond. Though it could be and was at times misused, our sexual contact with one another brought us emotionally closer as a group, making us less fearful of one another than men ordinarily are. As one man said, "It beats a handshake when it comes to getting to know another guy and figuring out if you can trust him."

We were already predisposed to the development of our caretaking abilities so as to feel needed and bolster self-esteem, and the sexual revolution brought us into intimate contact with one another in greater numbers than ever before. While still learning how to best make use of our sexuality with one another, sexual bonding increased our caring for one another. It added a slightly different meaning to the old truth that "in union there is strength."

The wave of sexual liberation had made us sexually conversant as a group. We were not as shy as the average citizen in admitting and discussing sexual feelings and behavior. Of course, it was our sexual friendliness as a community that made us a high-risk group for the new disease. But it was the same sexual ease and honesty that helped us quickly come to grips with the need to fight the disease in every possible way. We were able to disseminate the needed information, educate one another, and change sexual attitudes and behavior with unprecedented speed.

While scare tactics and dire warnings had not been effective in combating the spread of earlier life-threatening sexually transmitted diseases when there was no treatment or cure available, in this case something was different. Each of us was motivated not only by fear for our own safety, but also by our deeply ingrained desire to care for one another. And with both strong motivational factors operating, mutual support made it possible to accomplish the seemingly impossible task of changing sexual attitudes and behavior.

Our need to express love and caring was stronger than individual habits of sexual behavior. It might be less sensually satisfying or aesthetically pleasing to use a condom, but it certainly could be done if it would save lives. Whereas, with previous life-threatening sexually transmitted diseases, people were willing to gamble in order to have momentary sexual gratification, gay men were helped in learning more rational behavior because of the inherent conflict that is more clear for us. We dare not risk the lives of the people we care for, and we are inclined to care for the people to whom we are attracted. Our sense of safety in the world rests firmly on behaving as needed, caretaking people. It interferes with the normal state of sexual arousal to take a momentary gamble once we are aware of the possible consequences. It would not only mean risking exposure to disease in a passionate moment of arousal, but *risking our total sense of safety in this lifetime* by acting in a manner contrary to a caretaking orientation. To risk the life of someone we care for is to destroy our own sense of safety in this world. It is something we cannot afford to do.

With surprising speed, information was disseminated in cities where the disease was most rampant about sexual practices believed to present the greatest risk. It was an extremely success-ful educational effort. The information passed from person to person and sexual practices changed radically and quickly. The incidences of *all* sexually transmitted diseases among gay men plummeted. Caretakers were learning to take care of themselves and were taking care of one another.

The immediate dangers of the AIDS epidemic and the need for educational information have become clear. The absolute nec-essity of combating the disease in every possible way is clear. The disease is a threat to life for everyone. People have been less clear in understanding that it is the *disease* that poses the threat, not the people who have the disease.

The second epidemic, fear-based hysteria, may be more costly in the long run. Fear is a terrible threat to human life. Fear can cause a person to resist living. Fear can cause irrational be-havior. Fear can cause people to harm their neighbors. Fear can cause a person to deny reality. Worse, fear can generate fear. And fear can be used to manipulate other people.

We know the harm that comes from epidemics of fear. Rumor can cause fear that leads to a run on a bank, draining it of its reserves. A small, easily contained fire in a theater can cause fear that starts a stampede in which people are trampled to death. Irrational fear caused many United States citizens of Japanese an-cestry to be deprived of civil rights and worldly possessions and to be imprisoned during the Second World War. During that same period in human history, fear facilitated the ultimate horrors of Nazi concentration camps in Europe and the use of the atomic bomb in Japan.

As the AIDS epidemic spread to people other than gay males, it became newsworthy. The irrational behavior that is the hallmark of an epidemic of fear began at once. Some children had developed the disease as a result of blood transfusions with in-fected blood. Mobs of fearful parents demanded that these chil-dren be kept out of school, isolated, for fear that they would some-how infect their own children. People whose tested blood indi-cated that they had been exposed to the virus and had developed antibodies (and might or might not be incubating the virus in their blood) were fired from jobs, removed from the military, and punished because it was presumed that they were gay. Openly gay people were forced out of jobs and residences and denied insurance because it was presumed that they carried the virus. In San Francisco, Los Angeles, and New York City, gay groups repeatedly demanded state or federal legislation that would protect them from such discrimination in employment, housing, and insurance coverage.

Some secret and not-so-secret plans were proposed to isolate, quarantine, imprison, or exile people with AIDS, and even people who *might* develop AIDS. There would be no rational reason to do so. Such proposals were simple manifestations of irrational behavior in an epidemic of fear.

In the United States, it was revealed that a secret "scientific study" was about to be funded by the military that would "prove" that AIDS was spread by casual contact and that "possible carriers" should therefore be "isolated." Yet all real scientific evidence was continuing to demonstrate that AIDS was *not* spread by casual contact. No truly scientific study is ever undertaken with the result presumed to be known. To do so in the face of consistent scientific evidence supporting a contrary likelihood was absurd. It was a shocking attempt to use fear to deprive some citizens of their civil rights.

An epidemic of fear depends upon the assumption that *you* must be sacrificed in order for *me* to survive; *they* must be sacrificed in order for *us* to survive. We have confronted the shame of the aftermath of this assumption time after time in history. When the hysteria produced by fear subsides, we remember that there is no *them*. There is only *us*. When *some of us* are made to suffer, *we* suffer. If another individual, family, group, or nation is victimized this time, it becomes easier for you to be the victim the next time. The road is better paved with each irrational transgression of human rights.

A friend who was nearing the end of his battle with a series of illnesses resulting from AIDS said, "I am not afraid of my own dying. I guess some people do fear the unknown. For me, it's just the unknown. I feel sorry for the people who are afraid of living because they're afraid of the unknown in *living*. People who live their lives afraid and suspicious of other people don't do much living. The people who are afraid of me because I'm a person with AIDS have a worse disease than mine. I guess I'd like to help them, but they won't let me come close enough to help. They're going to die and I'm going to die — but right now I'm not afraid to live."

It seems likely that we will conquer this epidemic of AIDS, but will we ever conquer the recurrent epidemics of fear that are so damaging? There is no inoculation except an acquired ability to embrace the truth that we are one. We are a humanity, part of one human family, one system. To care for one another is to care for ourselves. When one of us is sick, we are sick. When one of us is harmed, we are harmed. When one of us is helped, we are helped.

I remember a spirited, fun-loving person at an AIDS fundraiser winking and saying, "Don't give until it hurts, honey, give until it helps — you."

Growing Old
in Twenty Years

Within two decades, we gay people have found our identity as a group. In this brief time we also have experienced our collective youth, maturity and old age. It is a unique phenomenon. The result has been a compacting of joy, sorrow and wisdom. It has been a powerful awakening.

Our contemporary sense of collective identity had a beginning in the 1960s. Much of the world was integrating the social change resulting from the Second World War. Rarely questioned social values had been called into question. Social inequities that had been accepted as traditional were challenged. The customary structure of power and privilege was no longer acceptable. Rulers were being replaced by leaders. The oppressed were pushing for a place in the sun.

As was true for many other groups with a common identity, people who had been made to suffer because of their natural homoerotic inclinations began to reach out to one another in order to gain the collective strength needed for social protest. The first leaders appeared along with the early public demonstrations.

The contemporary watershed for gay people came late in

June of 1969 in New York City. There had been demonstrations of protest earlier but none as spontaneous, large and long-lasting. The police who came to oust the patrons of the Stonewall Bar were surprised when its gay patrons did not, as usual, meekly follow orders and disappear into the night. Instead, the police found themselves barricaded inside the bar and calling for defensive reinforcements as the angry crowd of gays outside grew in number, beginning a protest that was to last for three days, capture the attention of the world, and become commemorated as the Stonewall Rebellion. The anniversary of that rebellion is now celebrated around the world as Gay Pride Week.

Like healthy adolescents, whatever our individual ages, we had notified the custodians of tradition that we were forging our own identity and would no longer be obedient children. Like adolescents, we would draw support from peers, making our own mistakes together as we charted our adaptive path into an unknowable future.

Adolescence is an energetic, joyous and painful period in life. We must leave the predictable past with little knowledge of self except what we have been told. Yet we must draw on these tentative suggestions of identity to make the experiments that will reveal identity based on the morality of lasting personal values.

We had been told that our identity is defined by our nonconforming sexual attractions, wishes, fantasies and behavior. We had been called homosexuals for the past hundred years. We began with the assumption that it was our sexuality that defined us. Those of us who had enjoyed heterosexuality also were assumed to be hybrids with varying degrees of purity of identity. We knew it was true that our societies had relentlessly pushed us in the direction of heterosexuality.

Like the larger surrounding community, we failed to heed the evidence compiled by the Kinsey studies of the 1940s. Those studies confirmed that human sexuality, like most other human attributes, exists naturally on a continuum and is not an either/or choice. It is the very unusual individual whose natural inclinations are totally homosexual or totally heterosexual.

Approaching the freedom of our adolescence with the assumption that our previously forbidden homosexual inclinations formed the core of our identity, we lost no time in exploring these sexual interests. Our first civil rights demands were aimed at assuring our right to assembly so that we could find one another. Then, we needed the right to invite one another to participate in sex without the intimidation of entrapment by police. Next, we needed the right to safe places where we might select sexual partners and proceed with our sexual experimentation.

The strength of our tide was formidable. There were pockets of resistance in various places, but our places of meeting and sexual experimentation multiplied so rapidly in the Western world that most people accepted the phenomenon as if it had been there all along. Although the presumed purpose of our vastly expanding arena (developing in a period of general sexual liberation) was sexual commerce, it provided the opportunity to find one another and admit feelings of general attraction.

Sexuality is not isolated from the rest of our being. As we found one another, we mutually reinforced one another's natural desires for lovemaking and caretaking. Confused by the sexual commerce of the time, the lovemaking and caretaking often seemed secondary, but the strength of these needs forced us to pay attention to them. Though we subjected one another to rejection, in imitation of competitive heterosexual mating rituals, we felt the hurt and wrongness in the experiences.

While the focus remained on winning the sexual competition by being found sexually desirable, we quickly saw that the game was hollow (though it continued, rewarded by the more real secondary gains of finding one another and forming bonds). Last year's lover became this year's friend. We helped one another across social barriers of national boundaries, education, ethnic identity, and social class. Our caretaking and lovemaking developed strong roots.

It began to become clear that the larger community was, as it always has been, much more uncomfortable with our *lovemaking* than with the sexual behavior that presumably had been so objectionable. Sex palaces were licensed; marriage was not. Neither church nor state would condone lifetime gay marriages. Nor was it considered seemly for us to hold hands or show obvious affection in public at any time! With hindsight, we can see that this might have been anticipated. Institutions of all sorts had for centuries looked the other way regarding homosexual behavior. It flourished in boarding schools, prisons, mental hospitals, the military, religious orders, and all sorts of respectable clubs. But it has been understood always that it was to be discreet: there was to be no hint of real love in the "making" and no hint of lifetime commitment to someone of the same gender based on surrender to affection. Sex could be tolerated, bonds of love could not.

Committed love that could grow in time — real lovemaking between people of the same gender, particularly between men — threatened the established power structure. Men had to be prepared to fight one another when ordered to do so or their rulers felt insecure in their power. The greatest anxiety was experienced by guardians of established tradition as gay people in the military and the clergy began to come out of the closet. Hundreds of variations on a familiar theme were witnessed. "They awarded me medals for killing men but imprisoned me and gave me a dishonorable discharge for loving one."

The truth began to grow in us. We gay people had been found guilty of being sinful, mentally ill, and criminal by family, friends and community — not because of sexual feelings or behavior but because they had been frightened by any hint of our desire to love and make love with one another.

Thus threatened, living in danger, we developed our caretaking abilities so as to be needed and find a relatively safe niche in society. Ironically, many of us had used our caretaking needs to become the priests, soldiers, and other caretakers of the established social order. Some of us had become our own jailers.

I remember the awful realization coming to one man during a gay group psychotherapy weekend. He had entered religious life early to atone for his presumed sinful nature. He found too much temptation to love during his years there, so he left and entered the military. There he found undeniable love with a comrade. He saw his lover shot thirty feet away from him during combat, and heard the screams of agony and despair in his lover's final moments of life. After leaving the military he became a mental hospital professional. When he awakened to the roles he had played in repressing his own natural love and love of other gay people, the pain he experienced was excruciating.

In the 1970s our maturation was visible. We engaged in dialogue, confrontation, and struggle when required, with the rulers of church and state who declared us criminal, mentally ill and sinful because of our need to love. We were elected and appointed to public office, demanded legislative change, challenged immigration laws, and successfully demanded a sane revision of mental health diagnostic guidelines. Not only did we see to it that laws were changed, we entered the legislatures and became judges and members of police forces as openly gay people prepared to alter prejudice based on ignorance.

We became increasingly visible in all walks of life as we disclosed gay identity to family and friends. We were growing up and were serving notice that we would no longer tolerate the condescending pretense that sexual preference had anything to do with respectability and the full rights of citizenship. We were beginning to understand that our loving threatened the established social order. We had become vital caretakers in that social order. The time was at hand for the social order to change. We would no longer serve as its obedient slaves. Our societies would have to change to include us and our loving as a recognized vital part of society. Community values were overdue for change. We were not the only group that had been held down too long.

Our rapidly developing maturity was evident in our open participation in the arts and the social service programs of the 1970s. In San Francisco, Jon Simms brought a huge, stylish, and spirited Gay Freedom Day Marching Band and Twirling Corps into the streets, winning prizes in diverse community parades and inspiring pride as they burst into their familiar theme: "If the folks back home could see me now..." Other gay bands emerged immediately in other cities.

It was Jon who started a gay men's chorus, a lesbian and gay choral group, a chamber music group, and mixed musical celebrations, all quickly followed by similar musical groups.

Writers published respectable fiction and non-fiction works that explored facets of our identity and were displayed in the windows of major bookstores rather than being stocked under the counter in small specialty shops. Authors were interviewed by newspaper columnists and listened to on radio and television talk shows. They were viewed as respectable people with unorthodox but respectable views.

Artists had openings in public galleries, displaying work that explored our aesthetics. Playwrights were able to have their honest work performed in major theaters as they helped audiences look at our lives seriously. And, in a sure sign of our acceptance (if not appreciation), lesbians and gay men began to appear in small incidental roles in films and on television. We had become visible and sometimes entertaining.

Scholars began to write about us and investigate our history. Slowly, the academic world began to admit that it had hidden the gay identity of many of the heroes and heroines of history. Forbidden poems by Shakespeare, Whitman and other respected poets found their way into print. Biographies of world leaders who had worked for social reform began to make passing reference to gay identity. Our history began to emerge.

But maturation is not tidy — especially the maturation of a group so rich in its individual differences. As the general thrust of our maturation moved into civil rights, religion, politics, the arts and social service, more gay men and lesbians were newly "coming out" every day. And they were of all ages and from every walk of life. More than once I was surprised by a grandparent who has sought help because she was about to come out to sons, daughters and grandchildren. Of course young adults, old enough to face parental displeasure without fear of incarceration or other direct punishment, were also emerging daily and wanting to know where to find the liberation party.

As a community, we continued to explore the sexual aspects

of our identity. While many of us had come to realize that we were more than sexual beings, we knew it was important to find our truthful sexuality also. There was some pressure within our community to develop a party line based on a simple assumption that all sex is good and more sex is better. And there was some contrary pressure to pretend that we were as piously puritanical as the least sexual (and therefore least sinful) people in the world were presumed to be. Because of the wonderful, chaotic variety of individuals embraced by our diverse community, we managed to avoid throwing out the baby of sex with the cleansing bath water of debate. There was more than enough support for individuals to continue to explore their own individual sexual needs and their satisfaction in a wide variety of forms. We had a long history of being harassed with the presumed "rights" and "wrongs" of sexuality. As a community, we were determined to be tolerant and respectful of individual differences.

That tolerance continued to produce experimental behavior that shocked, amused and instructed. Since recreational (psychotropic) drugs were in vogue in the larger community, drug experiences became a part of the sexual experimentation for some. Since communal living was part of the experimentation in the larger community, group sex and multiple relationships became a part of the sexual experiment. It was not unusual to be introduced to two people with the words, "This is my lover, Michael, and this is my boyfriend, Fred." Or one might be introduced with, "These are my lovers, Cynthia and Maxine."

One popular joke at the time was to ask why most socially correct people did not care for group sex. The answer was there were too many thank-you notes to write!

History will tell us which of the sexual experiments, if any, proved dangerous, and which proved useful and durable. Like all social experimentation, answers will become more clear only in the future. The important fact is that we were able to struggle free of the restriction of being defined by sex while still remaining open to the search for satisfying and socially viable sexuality.

With the continued development of our collective maturity,

as we examined our values and refined our morality, we used the word *commitment* more and more. We had been denied the encouragement and sanctions of church, state and community in making commitments based on our love and caring, but we were now able to offer that support to one another.

Our social service programs grew in diversity and strength. We offered legal help to people who were in trouble with the law because of their gay identity. We offered emotional support groups, psychotherapy and counseling to gay people in need. We developed outreach programs to help gay senior citizens, particularly those who were socially isolated or poor. We offered help in finding nondiscriminatory housing. We funded efforts to help gay parents with custody problems resulting from gay identity. We developed outreach programs to young gay and lesbian runaways. We formed support groups for gay teens, gay fathers, lesbian mothers, gay and lesbian alcoholics and other substance abusers, gay and lesbian clergy and religious community members, parents of lesbians and gays, and support groups for every imaginable profession including physicians, lawyers and psychologists. There were even gay business groups developed and gay banks that vowed to help lesbians and gay men find nondiscriminatory home mortgages.

Another indicator of the continuing maturation in the lesbian and gay community was the development of various interest groups where we could meet on a basis other than visual appraisal of potential sex partners. Gay people formed baseball and football teams, bowling clubs, hiking clubs, travel clubs, language study groups, literature courses, political clubs, investment clubs, theatrical groups and gardening and cooking classes. We had become a grown-up community by the beginning of the 1980s.

Perhaps the most solid evidence of our secure maturity was our willingness to integrate with the non-gay world. We had uncovered enough of our own identity to earn that security. But we made it clear that we were interested only in mutually respectful integration. We would not be covered and hidden away. Charity benefits, where a gay baseball or football team played the police or firemen's team, were fine. Admission to a national contest of choral groups *only if* "gay" were deleted from the group's name was not acceptable. It was as simple as that. We offered cooperation in worthwhile community events but were not available for condescension. We welcomed non-gay people in our gatherings and expected the same welcome in theirs.

Then, very early in the 1980s, the AIDS epidemic began to show itself in the gay community and elements of old age appeared in our new maturity. Suddenly, like a community of old people, many of us were obliged to guard our health zealously, to nurse our ailing friends and kin, and to supply a new array of health programs. Suddenly, we were attending funerals and memorial services for friends who had been young and healthy a year earlier. Suddenly, we were scanning the obituaries for the names of our peers.

This was the second watershed, the second turning point that helped us to understand our identity. Just as the police had expected us to run from them and from one another when they raided the Stonewall in June of 1969, the world expected us to flee from one another in the face of this deadly epidemic. But we did not. Instead, once again, we gathered together to help one another. Our caretaking abilities already were developed, ready for use in this expression of our love and caring for one another.

By the time this second watershed came, we knew and trusted our loving enough to expect no less of ourselves as a group. While some individuals might be frightened away, together we knew ourselves to be strong and reliable in our loving. Once again our loving threatened the guardians of the established social order, but we trusted our strength.

We do not know why any person loves. But we know now that we gay people begin our lives ready to love easily. It is this facet of our nature that threatens the conformists. We recognize our feelings of attraction to other people and know that these feelings go far beyond sexual appetite. When we are attracted to another person, we offer our care and our vulnerability. When the attraction is mutual, the combined offering creates that special bond of love. Sexuality may be a component, but the bond is basically spiritual in nature. If our attraction is mutual, and not damaged by our surroundings, it will create the state of love in which my happiness is enhanced by yours, my sadness deepened by yours, my sense of well-being completed by yours. And this state of love is elastic. It can embrace and shelter many people.

As we quickly set about to love and care for one another in the face of AIDS, we were rewarded by added clarity about our nature. Because of the early suspicion that the disease was transmitted by sexual contact, we were obliged to review our sexual behavior immediately. We did not want to harm ourselves or one another.

We learned to forego sexual pleasures if necessary, if that self-denial meant being better able to share our love and caring for one another. We had no real choice but to relearn our sexual behavior in any way necessary. Contrary to the myth that had been the core of our identity as we were understood in the world, sex was *not* the most important facet of our identity. Our loving and caring appeared to be the central facets, with sexuality being no more than one possible good way to express that love and care, whether profoundly or in play.

Finally, we were gaining freedom from the myth. We are not people driven by sex. We are people strongly motivated to love and care. We have the same sexual needs that any people have, no more and no less.

But, partly because of the myth, we had developed a community tradition of being non-phobic about sex. We had become a sexually friendly, sexually tolerant group, now ready to make the necessary changes in sexual behavior. Our need to love and care and our greater comfort with human sexuality made the change in sexual behavior more possible for us. It would be a much more difficult change to accomplish in the larger community because there, sex presents a massive approach-avoidance conflict, a taboo that leads to secret preoccupation. And that which is very secret is very difficult to change.

With the gift of added self-awareness came a temporary

danger. Our youth, maturity and old age had all happened in less than two decades. There was a possible pitfall. We had to be careful not to deny our sexual ease and sexual friendliness. Twenty years earlier, we had been led to believe that all that we had in common was desire to use one another sexually. Since our sexual behavior now seemed to pose a health risk and we knew our loving and caring to be more important to us, it would be possible for the pendulum to swing the other way and find us denying the gift of sex to one another. In our search for safe and healthy change in sexual behavior, we had to remind one another that sexual behavior needed to be changed but not abandoned. We had to remind one another that it was a virus, not sex, that was killing our friends. To deny the basic goodness of our sexual caring for one another would be to jump back into the confusing days of our collective youth when sex was not yet seen in perspective.

Now, knowing ourselves to be a loving and caring community, confronted during a mere two decades with all the problems of youth, maturity and old age, we found ourselves increasing the strength and pace of our spiritual search. It had started in the years of our collective maturity. As we caught glimpses of our obscured history, we saw that the spiritual realm had been very important to our gay ancestors. We knew that our coming together in these two decades had provided spiritual experiences for many of us, but we had hardly begun to articulate our unasked questions.

Now we found ourselves surrounded by pain and death. Our ability to love and care helped us. But how could we learn to feel the pain and death, experience it, accept it, love, care, appreciate life and move forward?

Any person who is committed to loving and caring is no stranger to pain or to joy. We are not misty-eyed romantics who feed on denial of reality. We know that the human experience is a balanced package. We know the feel of bleak times, yet we know that *despair is as false as euphoria.* We know the reality of death. We who love and care learn that the only choice possible for us is full commitment to life for as long as life lasts.

Caretaking involves assuming a fair share of responsibility for the well-being of life in all its forms. In order to do this we must develop a foundation of thoughtfully examined values.

Responsibility begins with the self. Each of us has the responsibility of caring for the development and health of our own intellect, emotions and body. Each of us must find our own sense of purpose in life and find a place in the integrated, changing balance of life. We are responsible for tending the life we have. Body, mind, and spirit are our basic assets.

Part Three
CHANGING

States of Awareness

We love. We care. We change. We humans are able to achieve conscious awareness of our relatedness to one another, to other animals, and to all other forms of life. We are able to develop skills that permit us to articulate and communicate our conscious awareness to one another. We are able to assimilate the conscious awareness that our ancestors left for us in their words, music and other products, and by their evolving realizations, attitudes, and social customs. We today leave this same communication of conscious awareness for the evaluation and use of those who come later.

Change is as seamless and vast as time. Conscious awareness of our changing place in life, together and individually, permits the sense of orientation that is required if one is to experience inner peace in this lifetime. Each of us is no more than a stitch in a vast fabric, or a cell in the organism of life, yet each of us yearns for understanding of our place as we and the whole continue to change. Everything that we know anything about is changing. Our bodies are changing while the continents and seas of this planet change amid the constant shifting movement of change in the heavens around us.

Sometimes there is a triggering event that we notice because it suddenly alters the direction or intensity of change. An accident leaves a person physically handicapped and the course of that person's life is altered. The New World was discovered and the course of European civilization changed forever. The first satellite sailed out beyond the atmosphere of the earth, settled into orbit, and the course of the world was changed, as it was by the explosion of the first atomic bomb, and the invention of the silicon chip.

Difficult as it is to confront the phenomenon of constant change with conscious awareness, superimposing some sort of map can help one's perception. Philosophers and psychological theorists have used the notion of "stages" or "phases" for centuries. It is a device that permits one to look at smaller segments of the whole and see how the segments are related.

.Theorists sometimes speak of stages, phases, passages, and seasons of life. These ways of viewing can aid not only in the understanding of how the segments of the whole are related, but in charting one's course.

As a person who has listened to stories and observed the development of conscious human awareness for several decades, I am aware of patterns. While there is no single ideal pattern, we can superimpose a see-through map on change process and use it as an aid in comprehension. One might think of a map with seven segments, though it could as easily have more or fewer segments. (I try to avoid the use of the words *phase* and *stage* because so many people continue to believe that a phase is a passing phenomenon of little importance and that stages are steps, with Step One leading to Step Two.) I prefer to think of the segments of a map of human conscious awareness as *states*. We are accustomed to the idea of moving freely from one state to another, even if there is a general overall direction to the movement.

It is not only individuals who move through these states of awareness as they experience change; groups of people do so also. Some unfortunate people are unable to remain alert and grow as they experience change; they visit fewer states. Fear and private insecurities can impede conscious exploration, and the result is a life less rich, limited both in scope and depth.

The seven states that I suggest here are: Conception, Darkness, Blinding Light, Necessary Contradiction, Commitment, Sacrifice, and Balance. Named in that order, they suggest a pattern of evolution. But individuals move from one state to another in unique patterns, often revisiting one state or another before moving on to a new one. The general direction is toward Balance, a state we all desire.

While these states can describe the flow of a lifetime, they may also be used to describe the conscious awareness of change experienced in a day or an hour. It is not an unusual day that finds one moving through the states of Darkness, Balance, Necessary Contradiction, and back to Balance again — if fortunate. It is not pleasant to end one's day out of balance.

CONCEPTION

All stories are about change and every story has a beginning. But where does the story begin? Usually it begins with a glimpse at one particular moment in the flow of change.

New comes from old which was once new. The well-rooted young tree was seeded by that bit of life yielded by its mature ancestor. The rain that is drawn from the sky, meeting the surface of the planet, was drawn to the sky as moist vapor from the same surface.

And how does the life of a new human being begin? A complex drama involving two people leads to the meeting of two cells. As each cell moves towards the other, the unique combination forms a single cell. In that merger, the individual identity of each of the previous two cells is lost forever. Each of the two original cells was the unique product of the union of two other unique individual cells.

A man I met recently is the father of a son who loves another man's son. The man told me, "It doesn't seem to bother the other boy's father so much and I'll be damned if I know why. I cannot conceive of such a pairing! I cannot conceive of such an abomination being called *love*." He used the word conceive again and again. He cannot conceive. It is the truth. His mind is neither fertile nor is it receptive. When his habitual style of understanding finds a way to open and permits old ideas to be penetrated by other ideas, he will conceive. Only then will he nurture new ideas that are unique, coming in part from what he already knew and in part from the "other" that found a way into his awareness.

There are many times in human history that one could cite as points of conception. World War II was an awful time during which a rich variety of social changes were conceived. Amid the changes, there was the persistent human search for love and understanding. Individuals from different social backgrounds, different national traditions, and amazingly different cultures met and explored one another. New views mated with those that had been established and unquestioned. New social perspectives grew from the mating. Patriotism and war, for instance, were questioned. Two decades later, people were in the streets of the world protesting traditional social conventions such as the necessity of war and the presumed moral right of the more powerful to oppress those less powerful.

The people ordered to kill, destroy, and risk their own death, and those seemingly helpless people who loved them, began to question whether they were being sent into war to protect that which they valued and those whom they loved or if they were sent as mere disposable weapons, protecting the property and lives of their masters. The right of one person to control the destiny, quality and length of life of another person was sharply called to question in new ways, and the social ramifications continue to unfold today.

In hundreds of ways we are now asking difficult questions that demand new answers about when a person needs to be "represented." A person can be the legally helpless victim of a presumed "representative," who in fact acts as the person's lord and master. Who has the right to speak for the very old and infirm, the child, the mentally retarded, or the person in extreme economic poverty?

In this atmosphere of social questioning, a wave of liberation groups gathered momentum. Blacks, women and other groups demanded full civil rights in some nations. Homosexuallyoriented speakers dared step from invisibility to ask, "Who says that we are inferior or to be treated as second-class citizens? And who dares grant that person authority to make this judgment that subjects us?"

Minds conceived new thoughts and new questions. "Why is prejudice accepted and permitted to ruin lives?" "Why have parts of history been suppressed?" "Why have we been imprisoned, tortured, and exterminated?" "On whose authority are we branded and to whom does *that* person answer?"

Those days, like these, were daring, heady times. I remember seeing the first issue of a new magazine called *GAY* on a newsstand three times before having the courage to purchase a copy. I was a college professor and a married man with children; someone might see me. It took more weeks to find the courage to telephone the publishers and volunteer to contribute an article.

The questions of the day had begun to reach into my mind. I reviewed my training as a clinical psychologist and I reviewed the professional literature. I saw that my training had tricked me. The professional pronouncements about homosexuality were nothing more than opinion based on prejudice. The small amount of real evidence pointed to homosexuality as being a natural variation within the normal range of human sexual attraction. It harmed no one, though the prejudice of some professionals had spun a web of fear. New thoughts were taking root as a result of my conception.

A boy in an elementary school for gifted children, where I volunteered as the school psychologist, told me, "I don't see why my mother and my father tell me I should love both of them when they hate each other so much. They won't see one another or even talk to one another."

My mother, ending her days in an Intensive Care Unit, held my hand and looked deeply into my eyes. She could not speak. Why had her life been so difficult every step of the way, as she worked to exhaustion to make life better for her family? Could it be that she had been too unquestioning of what she had been told to believe from the days she started work in a factory at nine years of age? Conception comes at any age and any time. My mother had visited many states of consciousness already in her years and was daring some final exploration, preparing for death.

Last week an eighteen-year-old friend of the family told me, "All I care about is getting away and having my freedom." I asked what he needed to get away from and how he imagined his freedom would be. How did he imagine he would use his independence?

"I'll get a car, a job and an apartment. I'll be on my own." That was as far as his conception had carried him. The answers to my questions had not yet formed. New thoughts were meeting old.

I think sometimes that the state of Conception must be the state of awareness in which pre-verbal babies dwell and the state of conscious awareness in which Van Gogh lived. Innocent receptivity is awesome. The incongruity between this state and the ways in which the world is seen by those who dare to officially define reality is painful. But we all know that, or we once did.

DARKNESS

Individually, and in groups, each of us has lived in our own periods of darkness. As a state of awareness it is difficult to remember later, when we are no longer in it, because the memories of it carry so much hurt and anger. So much of it is forbidden. There are the memories of being told not to feel what you felt, not to see what you saw, and not to think what you thought.

Everyone is certain to have visited this state of awareness as a young child learning to communicate. You feel anger and you are told, "You're cranky and tired. Go take a nap and don't let me hear another word from you until you are in a better mood." Of course, it is not difficult to translate that command to, "Do not feel or express anger except when you are told it is permitted and safe. Anger is unacceptable and dangerous. Call the emotion by another name and do what you can to forget it."

Truth is under siege in this state of awareness. Many people, perhaps most, are so bound to convention by their own feelings of anxiety, dimly rekindled whenever they are confronted with naked truth, that they painfully teach their young not to see.

For the child learning to communicate with words, everything is categorized as neatly as possible. If there is a gray area in the sea of black and white, it is one shade of gray only. "Let's play a game. See if you can guess if it is animal, vegetable or mineral." If you were naive enough to ask, "Which of the three is the sky?" probably you were shamed with patronizing laughter. Wide-ranging truth, with all its unnamed nuances, is squeezed into uncomfortable categories in this state.

These are our first lessons in how to break the whole into two parts and think of them as opposites. Is it good or bad, right or wrong, beautiful or ugly, sweet or bitter, love or hate? You are instructed that certainly you cannot love and hate the same person. And how could something be both beautiful and ugly? Innocent truth insists that it is not only possible but necessary. You know it happens constantly. Convention instructs, however, that such a notion is foolish, abnormal and dangerous. "Don't touch that thought! You'll get hurt!"

So depleted are some of us by our battle between inner truth and outer conventions, that we withdraw to an "acceptable" life with a very low profile, living out our days with tiny pleasures and very little overt passion, rarely able to remember even our dreams.

My office used to be ten blocks from my home. It was an uphill walk going home, but I used it as a way of clearing my mind, letting the details of the day fall away. One autumn evening I left the office just as the sun had set. There was a hint of chill in the air and I could see migrating birds high above the city's buildings. A few blocks along I was stopped by a woman who looked to be no more than in her mid-forties, yet already her posture had begun to bend.

"Are you walking up the hill?" she asked.

"Yes."

"You look like a nice man. Would you mind if I walk along with you? It gets a little scary for a woman alone in the city when it starts to get dark."

Remembering the con games I have heard and read about, I

made a mental note to keep my wallet close to my person. "Not at all," I responded. "How far are you walking?"

"Just four-and-a-half blocks. You can almost see the house from here. It's that green one with the dark roof, just up the hill?"

I did not see it, but I nodded just to be reassuring.

"Are you returning home from work?" she asked pleasantly.

"Yes, I am. Are you?"

"Oh, heavens no. Not at this hour. I've just been to church service. I manage to get there at least once each day and I feel better if I can make it twice."

"That's nice," I said. What else can one say? To inquire even as to denomination might seem an invasion of privacy.

"What sort of work do you do?" she asked after a small silence.

"Oh, dear, here it goes," I thought. I hedged for a moment, knowing my need to tell the whole truth would win out. "I'm a writer . . . and . . . psychologist."

"A psychologist! How interesting!"

I braced myself. Only two-and-a-half more blocks.

"Are you one of the kind that has people look at ink blots and tell you dreams?" she asked.

That was better than I had been expecting. "Yes. Sometimes I do. It depends on the person."

"Well, I never dream." She said it as if I had accused her of wearing scarlet silk underwear. "Never!" A moment of silence. "But then, what is there to dream about?" She smiled. "I think if you lead a clean, decent, Christian life, keep evil thoughts out of your mind, and read the Bible when you're in doubt, that about takes care of things, don't you?"

"I never thought about it quite that way," I answered honestly.

She seemed pleased. Another small silence. "Well, think about it. I guess I'm what they call a loner — a real frontier gal. Plain life is good enough for me. I never could understand what gets people so wrought up that they have to come see people like you. No offense, of course. Well, here's my house. Hope you have a nice walk home."

She apparently had failed to notice or had forgotten that someone had painted her green house pale gray with white trim. It was a lovely old Victorian with the small detail paint done in violet and gold. I hope she does notice it sometime and that it *is* her house. I confess that I wondered if her prayers were as well laundered as her dreams were erased. Such discipline!

Darkness is the confusing dim state of awareness visited when a person is feeling "down". A battle rages between the colorful full array of truthful passions storming within, seeking release, and the seemingly stronger, containing, static force of conformity that stands guard in the immediate environment. One can almost hear the voices of childhood. "How dare you..." "You should be ashamed..." "Behave yourself this minute..." These words are the key to the fears that seal the inner prison of repression. With the prison sealed, one shuts down, breaking full diplomatic relations with the world.

We are taught that to dare to be conscious of all inner truthful feelings is to risk having those feelings move rapidly into "crazy," unacceptable, dangerous behavior that will hurt someone. And if someone is hurt, it is you who will suffer most, you are taught, because of inescapable guilt and punishment.

The real truth is that the reverse is the case. The more aware you are of your feelings, the more options are open to you and the more conscious you can be in making choices about whether or not to express feelings in behavior. The more conscious you are, the more responsible you can become.

People who have been successful in totally repressing feelings of murderous anger are the people most likely to be pushed past their limit and unexpectedly embark on a bloody rampage of murder for no apparent reason. The repressed feelings within become too compacted if there is no safety valve to prevent the explosive behavior.

It is the seemingly asexual family man who is most likely to fall into the trap of forcing family incest of some sort. It is the most loyal, subservient, and devoted corporate employee who is likely to take a suitcase packed with corporate profits on a one-way ride. It is the devout person who has lived a life unblemished by sin who is likely to enjoy the secret orgasmic pleasure of administering "necessary" torture to force a sinner's confession.

A fellow psychologist once told me that early in his career he had learned not to turn his back on anyone who told him repeatedly in the first meeting that he was a pacifist by nature. I might add that when a political leader repeatedly assures the world that his primary interest is world peace, I pay close attention to his budget for weapons. A repressed adult living fearfully in the state of Darkness shows his secret by indirection, but shows it often. There is little else that he knows, little else to show.

For each of us, fearful or not, there is the urge to move along to another state. There is the desire for release and the urge to find the peace of Balance. Some, like the devout loner, the incestuous father, or the torturing inquisitor, may be trapped in the state of Darkness for life, revisiting Conception at moments, catching a glimpse of the states of Blinding Light or Necessary Contradiction across the borders, tempted but fearful, hurrying back to the familiar limiting illusions of safety in the unremembered dreams of Darkness.

There are people like the young boy in the school for gifted children who begin their journey early in life, the need to understand being strong enough to overcome fear. Others, like my mother, facing death in the Intensive Care Unit, may have visited most states repeatedly, only to return through Darkness to Conception near the end of life with one last wish to leave fear behind and plunge with all strength left toward the state of Balance.

And there are the many, like the eighteen-year-old wanting independence while unsure what it is, who stand poised for the moment, one toe over the border, getting set, ready or not, determined to enter the next state and leave consideration of consequence to later.

A society's oppressed groups spend much of life in the state of Darkness until events conspire to make the time ripe. Conception is revisited, strength and leaders are produced, and the movement begins. Against all odds, facing threats to life itself, the journey to another state is under way. Oppression is too confining.

BLINDING LIGHT

The person may leave the state but the state does not leave the person so quickly. As you enter new territory, you bring learning and experience with you. It is altered, of course, by new experiences and learning. If Darkness contained the illusion of safety, Blinding Light contains the illusion of freedom. When this state is entered, a person imagines that the key to the candy store is firmly in hand. It feels as if one is free to feel and do anything and everything (as long as one is careful not to get caught by "authorities"). Any needs that have gone unmet and any appetite unsatisfied will now be satisfied in this new day of plenty. But the person is to learn that needs can be more than satisfied and appetite sometimes fed beyond desire.

As the child often lived in Darkness, the emerging adolescent often lives in Blinding Light. Perhaps it takes a ruthless, if temporary, insensitivity to smash across a border imagined to be so formidable. It is a time when it is easy to hurt people close to you. In light that is so bright, more is seen than ever was dreamed, but the intensity of the light obscures subtleties, some yet to be confronted.

A few years ago a young man sat in my office weeping. He recently had been released from a large state mental hospital on a work-furlough program, doing simple labor for minimum wage and living in a tiny room in the least desirable and most dangerous section of the city.

"I was doing okay," he told me. "I was a freshman in college, I was away from home and on my own. I was doing enough studying and I had a part-time job in the bookstore at school. I was a little scared, but so were most of the kids, I think. I knew I was making it." He took a deep breath and examined my face, probably hoping he could trust me.

"My family got all caught up in this big psychological fad

thing where you go to these giant meetings to find out all kinds of things about yourself. They get you to use their words, and push you to let out all your secrets. Everybody yells and cries and does these psychological exercises. The people running it keep telling you how they love you and how everybody supports you."

He searched my face again. "You know what I mean?"

I told him I was familiar with the group and its format.

"Well, it seemed to do my folks a lot of good and they kept calling me long distance and telling me I should go to one of those weekend meetings here and that they'd pay for it. So I figured there was nothing to lose and I signed up for a weekend. They got us all to play it their way and spill our guts. My secret was that I was gay. Everybody gave me lots of support and told me I was beautiful and that they loved me after I stood up and said it into a microphone. I got really high. It was the first time I had told anybody and here was this whole mob telling me it was great. One of the leaders said I should go right to the telephone on the next break and call my family and tell them."

He squeezed his eyes closed and grimaced, holding back feelings that came with the memory. "I bought it. I was high as a kite. I really thought I could do anything and everything would be fine. Well, I went to the phone and called. My family came down on me like a ton of bricks. They told me I was sick and that I should go back in and tell everybody what a rotten, sick pervert I was. I did it. I told everybody what my folks had said. And then some of the people were saying maybe I just thought I was gay and maybe I should try women. And other people were telling me to stand my ground because I was beautiful."

Sobs overtook him and it was a minute before he could continue talking. "I bought it. I was confused so I bought all of it. I bought everything everybody was saying, and I just cracked right down the middle. The next thing I remember is waking up in the city hospital and then being sent to the state hospital after a few weeks. That was two years ago."

His stay in the state of Blinding Light had been a brief and very painful day. Seldom is the stay that brief — though seldom is it without pain. He found his footing and moved along on his way to other states, wiser but bearing scars from the experience. As he told me, "Mostly I'm here because I want to make sure that I've picked up all the pieces and can get going with my life again. I don't want that kind of trip anymore if I can avoid it, but maybe I'd better learn to watch out where I'm going."

And there is a man who stands on a street corner in New York City, arriving every day just a few minutes before five o'clock in the afternoon to shout into the tired faces of the people emerging from the subway as rush hour gets under way. "I saw the light!" he shouts and gesticulates. "I saw it. You all can be free. Just throw down those chains and be free. Just stop working. Just quit and get on unemployment, food stamps, and welfare. All you got to do is pass the word along. Let the people who ain't seen the light do the work and the worry."

And there is the polite, well-dressed older woman who knocks on my door every few weeks to inquire if I am ready to come to Jesus and be saved yet. "It's so simple you know." She smiles patiently. "He will carry all of your burdens." She hands me a pamphlet and rings the next doorbell.

A former Yale student, turned ardent activist, recently appeared at a fundraising dinner party. He made his nonverbal statement by wearing ostentatiously ragged jeans and aged sandals. He also announced, in response to no one's request, that he would contribute no money. After his soup dish had been removed, he buttered a small piece of baguette and said, "It's quite simple. If a few people are injured or killed when we bomb one of the headquarters of capitalism, or if millionaire parents are disturbed because we hold a son or daughter for a ransom that will feed hundreds of the poor, it's an insignificant price to pay in a war for equality and freedom."

And what a time the last decade was for those of us who considered ourselves activists. We wore buttons, shouted slogans, confronted bigots in unexpected places, and went on a mission of sexual freedom that was slowed only as we began to realize that we were misusing one another and ourselves too often. We had slipped into the trap of defining our identity and our freedom in direct reaction to the definitions of us that our oppressors had used to keep us in our place.

Most people enter the state of Blinding Light with a headlong rush, dashing from the claustrophobia of Darkness, greedy for all that life has to offer the senses. Answers seem simple, because the more complex questions are too subtle to be seen or have not yet presented themselves.

The wounded young man who wanted to pick up the pieces of his life had learned that he needed to understand the questions before accepting easy answers. The man trying to bring his answers to the working hordes of New York City probably has been broken by personal tragedy. Perhaps he clings to his simple problem and its simple solution because it would hurt too much to reconsider the problems he has put aside. And who would dare to judge him without knowing the inner turmoil that sends him to that corner each working day?

I assume that the nice lady who rings doorbells and passes out pamphlets has never tried to assimilate in her understanding the centuries of human blood shed by people who thought they had found Jesus and were slaughtering their fellow humans for Him. I doubt if she would like to join their club for eternity.

The smug, well-fed, iconoclastic young man clinging to his revolutionary doctrine will have time, I hope, to visit other states before damaging lives of people he does not know. He has yet to learn that destruction is not constructive.

And most of us older activists who have kept moving along, pushed by heirs who see us as too conservative or too radical, are visiting other states now. We need not turn on one another as some of us once did and we need not make it all so simple by identifying easy enemies as we once did. Our need is to find deeper questions and broader answers.

It is this realization now, that there are subtleties hidden in the Blinding Light, that permits us to search for the other questions and answers. It was the speed of flight from Darkness that propelled us painfully into unseen obstacles in our path.

The young man recently released from the state mental hospital, in a rare wry moment said, "I knew there was such a thing as growing pains, but I didn't know how bad they could hurt."

They are apt to hurt the person who is in the state of Blinding Light and hurt those near that person too. Until the blindness clears and the more varied texture of life can be seen, it is difficult to ease the pain. But pain carves a deeper chamber in consciousness, and in that chamber understanding grows.

NECESSARY CONTRADICTION

Until life asks the question, you cannot answer. Until you answer, you cannot know your self. If Conception is the state in which all new is formed, and Darkness is the state of confusing restriction, Blinding Light is the state in which truth too simple is found, and Necessary Contradiction is the state in which one discovers that truth is not simple.

A woman friend who is a poet, a widow with grown children who have recently become parents themselves, returned last year from an impressive world journey. We had a long evening of dinner and talk soon after her return.

"It gave me a wonderful opportunity to review this life I have known," she told me. "When Paul died in the plane crash and left me with three small children, it was a terrible loss and a great shock but, of course, I found reserves I didn't know I had.

"When Lisa entered adolescence and began her adventuresome wanderings, I literally worried myself sick. Nothing I did helped, except perhaps the worry. I think she needed that as a kind of security that let her know I was ready to help. But nothing I did seemed to me to be of much help.

"And then she wandered off to wherever, and for six years now I have not known if she is alive or dead. For the years before she left I tried to find answers, not yet knowing that my trying *was* the answer, because I did not yet understand the question."

Like this strong woman, I had known her daughter Lisa to be a talented, nonconforming person, looking into the corners of

life most people avoid. Experimentation had led to drug depend-
ence. That, coupled with her determined association with the
fringe members of society, led her into deep confusion. She managed to free herself from the grip of mind-altering drugs but continued to go her individual, secretive way, searching out the dark
social places and the people who inhabit them until she disappeared from home, leaving a very upset mother as well as her confused, hurt, angry and worried older brother and sister.

"When Paul and I were very young," my friend said, "even
on into the early married years, we were terribly scattered. Inci-
dents and flashes of emotion bombarded us from all directions,
making it impossible to focus. What a lot of frantic energy was
spent — in all directions! But I think it was less waste than prepa-
ration, don't you? We couldn't begin to see more clearly until we
needed to seek focus as a refuge."

She showed me a tiny, primitive wood carving of a bent old
person, head tilted back, peering into space, face impassive. "So
now I watch as my next generation stumbles through their confusion with every bit as little genuine sense of direction as we had.
Of course, it hurts to watch. And, with the miseries that exist elsewhere in this world, it looks contrived, self-indulgent, and unnecessary. But if agonies aren't forced on us, we create them because
we must, I guess. And we elders of the village, like this small
carved person, watch and hurt and nod our heads in recognition,
a little older and wiser, but unable to do more than recognize the
dangerous rapids the younger ones are traversing."

As I was preparing to leave at the end of the evening, I admired an autumn landscape that she had painted. She said, "It's
odd to realize that it's the very late October of my life so soon.
There are more pastels and muted colors appearing every day
among the vivid colors. It appears there are seasons within seasons. You know, there's that moment of spring and the hour of
summer in each October day now, just as there were the very
bleak moments of winter that appeared regularly in springtime.
At least my travels have helped me to learn that people everywhere find it necessary to bear everything that life brings them.

Holding the happy and the sad simultaneously builds inner strength. You see more as your vision becomes less acute, don't you think? Odd, isn't it?"

Once conscious of the contradictions in life, one continues to find more of them, but also to find ways to come to terms with them. A peaceful settlement is sought for conflicting forces. Sometimes the momentary rest of a truce yields perspective. Intuitively, a person works toward some change within the self that will permit tolerance, peace, rest and balance, as more contradictions and potential conflicts are recognized.

Last week I witnessed a street scene that was like a staged drama. The couple stood on the sidewalk on a sunny afternoon, seemingly oblivious to the sidelong glances of passersby. "I need to know," the vexed young woman said. "Do you love me or don't you? Are we lovers or not?"

Her companion reached to touch her. "I told you. The answer is 'yes.' I love you and I don't. But the more I feel like I love you, the more I want out."

Graphic visual symbols represent the centuries of human spiritual search for truth while in this state. Familiar to most of us today are the Christian Cross and the Star of David. The Cross is two lines that intersect, the Star of David two triangles that intersect. The intersection of opposing forces joins the two that would otherwise be separate and less. It is the picture of counterforce and contradiction, a possible problem balanced in harmony and strength.

The discomfort of moving from the state of Blinding Light into the state of Necessary Contradiction can be seen in many young adults. When one is in the state of Blinding Light with its simple truth, it is easy to be surrounded by people and immersed in interaction with them. When one enters the state of Necessary Contradiction, there is an awareness of loneliness within the crowd. Awareness of loneliness had been put aside, out of consciousness, but now it presents itself with vivid feelings. There is a wish for true closeness. Of course, that closeness seems potentially confining. And so we see the lovers on the street, balancing the fear of loneliness or loss with the fear of restriction that might damage a tender, newfound individual identity. Discomfort comes with recognition of the contradiction.

The elastic bonding of people must echo the contradiction each of us experienced at birth. Cramped, safe, and secure in the uterus, we pushed and found more space in a wide world where we were separate and alone. The needed freedom was accompanied by a sense of loss. It was the beginning of a conflicting search for closeness and a distaste for confinement.

How often each of us hears the conflicts of others. "I love her but. . ." (We need to say the conflicts to someone so that we can hear them better ourselves.) ". . . but she causes me such pain and worry and sadness. Sometimes it makes me cry and feel real hate." Yet this same person ". . . makes me feel so loved sometimes . . . gives me the only real sense of worth, dignity, and well-being that I have ever known. We are real companions. Only with her can I be myself, laugh and love without being self-conscious."

When a group moves into this state of consciousness, the contradictions are even more confusing because the group is composed of a variety of individuals, each in his own personal state of development. After a group spree of simple freedom, responsibility appears, seeming to block the course of that freedom. As with the growing individual, it is the perennial conflict between the wish for security and the wish for freedom, started at birth. The group usually begins its liberation with a freedom festival, but the party may end abruptly. Like the individual, the group finds responsibilities that must be assumed if security is to be built. Life presents its questions and the group must form its answer.

As gay liberation moved into the state of Necessary Contradiction, it was with the usual confusion and dissatisfaction. Gay people had been separated from the presumably more respectable members of society on the basis of sexual orientation, the forbidden admission of same-gender attraction. It was a device used to separate this group of "different" people for the usual purposes of oppressive scapegoating.

As gay people emerged in liberation, the civil right to be different in sexual attraction was asserted. Invisible millions of "different" people became increasingly visible. The previously forbidden sexual desires could be satisfied in the new abundance of visible partners, and with the protections of new civil rights. Many members of the group plunged into the suddenly available sea of sexuality. But dissatisfaction came to individuals as they felt like objects used for temporary satisfaction. After the initial romp, sexual playpens became less like refreshing meeting places for partners and more like cages offering only temporary escape from loneliness and sexual need.

Meanwhile, the disappointed and disenchanted began to form into new common-interest groups. Political action and other civic concerns, dancing, skiing, camping, religion, films, peer counseling, or foreign language study could become a primary focus for gathering and meeting other gay people — who might or might not also be interested in a relationship or sex.

The new community was on its way to explore another state of awareness. Then the tidal wave of illness hit. A sudden frightening plague changed the tempo and the scope of our developing awareness forever.

Life had asked its question. Our answer had been forming. Unexpected disaster demanded even more sudden change in response. The strength of our balanced contradictions was revealed in the process.

COMMITMENT

This state of conscious awareness is the difficult, painful turning point in life. There is no Santa, and teachers do not have the answers. Once you have learned that right and wrong can co-exist in the same action, assumptions must be questioned forever after. You remember what you once knew — that truth is found in your willingness to yield to your own inner awareness.

Responsibility is rooted in personal values and those values must be clear. The surrounding world constantly makes its demands; our inner world responds. *You* must choose your action. Even passivity or turning one's back is a form of action.

Bruce is a man whose integrity I have watched grow stronger with the passing years. He is in the middle years of his life now, a time of awareness of the breadth of life — its troubles and pleasures, large and small. Last year he wrote to me, telling a story about a day he spent on a remote winter beach with two friends.

"We've done it before. You know, just gone out there for the whole day to mull things over. There's so much beauty, yet it's harsh in its way, a no-nonsense kind of place. But then, you've seen it, so you remember probably.

"The tide was full when we arrived, so we sat on some rocks for a while. When the tide had gone out enough that there was some beach to walk on, I set off on my own. I never know what's going to come into my mind (or if anything will, for that matter) when I take one of those solo walks.

"The early winter storms had caused a lot of change — mud slides on the cliffs, some big trees down, even some hefty rocks tumbled. I started thinking about Abigail, and I guess about me, too. The words that formed in my mind were 'When you have love you do not need it. And when you need love you do not have it.' That's as far as my mind took it then, except for noticing how inherent that truth is for all of us.

"The three of us caught up with one another again, chatted, shared a bite to eat, and then stretched out on the sand. I guess we were all in an introspective mood. I don't mean we were grim, or anything like that. We laughed and had a good time catching up with one another. But David said, 'How long has it been since we three met?'

"None of us answered the question out loud. I was thinking that the question didn't have an answer. It is as if we have always known one another — and at the same time have yet to meet completely. You begin to see where my mind was that day.

"The tide was way out by then, and again I wandered ahead of the other two. It was glorious. The enormous clouds in the sky, the wind in the trees and grass, and the water on the sand and rocks, combined in a symphony worthy of Beethoven. The sun shone, the gulls called, and the air smelled as fresh as it must have when the first people came upon that beach.

"You remember there is a reef with tidepools, small villages of awesome subtle beauty and slow-moving life. With the tide out I could walk far out on the reef and see this wonderful, secret world.

"Before I knew it, hours had passed and the other two were far behind me. I had come almost to the end of the reef. Perhaps a hundred yards ahead of me, something lay on the reef. It was much too large to be a dead bird or a fish, too large even to be one of the small sharks that wash in sometimes. I thought, 'Oh God, someone's dog fell off the cliff and drowned.' It wasn't moving.

"I walked to it and could hardly believe my eyes. It was a baby seal, two-and-a-half or three feet in length, dead on the rock. I saw a few birds circling overhead, interested. It was strange, being that close to the baby seal. It had long, curved eyelashes, tucks in the sides of its head for ears, and whiskers of pale yellow with tiny balls of green at the end. Its white fur was spotted as the body tapered toward the tail.

"Of course, I felt bad that its life was gone, but the rules were clear. The birds and the next tide waited. I had squatted down very close to it. As I stood to leave, I could not believe what happened. The seal's eyes opened and it lifted its head a tiny bit from the rock. Can you imagine the shock? I thought, 'Oh no, it's been smashed on this rock and is still living.' Somehow I could not bear the thought of the birds getting it. It would be hours before the tide was in that far again.

"I ran back to tell the other two. They were equally distressed. It was too far from the water to have been left momentarily by its mother. The three of us might be able to carry it to the ocean, but our interference might cause it to bite us. Or it might thrash and cause us to drop it on the rock. There seemed to be no answer.

"But I found myself quickly returning to that animal. When I reached it, it was quiet, and I thought it must have died while I was gone. But, as I squatted near it, the head raised again and the eyes opened. I found tears coming to my eyes, and I began to talk as if it could understand me. 'I cannot leave you here to die alone,' I said. 'Move if you can. Please. And if you can't, I'll have to stay here with you.'

"I neither know nor care how many people would believe me, but at that exact moment, the seal turned itself over with a very mighty effort that left its whole body heaving for breath. From there on the experience was unlike anything I could have expected. My attention locked onto that small seal, and its attention was on me. The big dark eyes were open wide now, looking straight into mine. It could not see the ocean from its position on the reef, but somehow I was determined to try to talk it back to its home, where it might heal. Maybe there was a mother out there waiting.

"I talked, shouted, ranted and raved. I said things like, 'You must do it, you must try! I know it's hard but I am here with you and will help. Come! Now!' And I began backing off a few inches at a time in the direction of the nearest water. It moved! Maybe a few inches at first, and with great effort that left it heaving each time, but it moved! And that was repeated again and again, with lapses when its eyes would close and the head would be put down on the rock from the awful effort and what I imagined was lack of hope. It still could not see the water.

"But like a madman, I shouted, demanded and coaxed. 'You must come. Now! I'll help you. I'll stay with you, but you must! Please try! Come on, now!' I clapped my hands, knelt down, pleaded. The other two had come close enough to watch the spectacle without distracting or scaring the seal.

"We made it, that baby seal and I. Inches at a time. It took the better part of an hour. But finally, I stepped backward into the water, and by then it could see the water too. We had covered about seventy feet. The seal followed my path into the water as I continued to talk to it. I told it to call for its mother in the water, and if mother did not come, to stay in the safer shallow water of the pool formed by the outer barrier of the reef until it was healed. Even in the water, it kept its head up as if listening to me.

"And then I said goodbye, tears pouring down my face, hoping it would be safe. After I said goodbye, I took a few steps away and then turned to look. The head surfaced for a moment and the eyes looked at me. Then I retreated to land and the baby seal dove into its home. True. Every word of it. And forever now, I am connected to that life in the sea.

"I guess that moment when something inside me clicked into place and I knew I would not leave that young creature to die alone was the real moment of commitment. I think I know what that word means now. The whole experience left a deep impression on me."

As in Bruce's story, first experiences in the state of Commitment go beyond surprise. The experiences are stunning. You cannot say that you have weighed the pros and cons fairly and rationally. A decision is made in less than an instant. Asked later, the person who risked his life to save someone against all odds, or the person who stepped in front of the policeman's club to protect someone fallen in a demonstration, is apt to mumble something about having done what seemed right.

The secret is contained in the word *right*. From the subtle, complex web of values spun while a person is visiting the state of Necessary Contradiciton, comes an inner sureness, a sense of right. To act in a manner that is not consonant with that inner web of integrity would put the person at war within the self.

An experience in the state of Commitment is not to be confused with an act of conformity. A conformist is more apt to turn the political fugitive in to "authorities" because "it's required" or "it's the law." Even when confronted, such a person will respond with a superficial answer such as, "Well, you can't fight City Hall" or "My country, right or wrong, love it or leave it. It was my patriotic duty." The conformist has little concern with duty to self or humanity, because there is so little comprehension of interconnectedness.

The heroic stories that fascinate us in newspaper accounts — the person who enters a house in flames because she hears a voice inside, the nonviolent activist who will neither strike back nor turn back, the Annie Sullivan who is determined that a Helen Keller must communicate with the world at any cost, the ordinary citizen who dares to risk hiding an Anne Frank — all fascinate us with the potent hint of inner commitment and responsibility. The sureness comes from a place deep within, not in response to illusion, but to a better-developed sense of our place in the world, an intuition of our responsibility in contributing to balance.

This is easy to understand if you have lived in the state of Commitment; it is difficult to understand if you have not. This state, and the states of Sacrifice and Balance, are sometimes seen but rarely visited by a person who does not awaken fully during his lifetime. Illusion is less present in this state of conscious awareness than in the states described earlier, it exists only in the haunting dim suggestion that commitment may be an act of will.

SACRIFICE

Sacrifice seems an odd concept to people today. Why would I give from my self or my possessions unless forced by law or circumstance? Sacrifice is today equated with loss.

Living in the state of Commitment prepares a person for an understanding of sacrifice. Sacrifice does not mean that I lose what I need, though it may look that way to the bystander. Rather I rid myself of the *unneeded* in order to gain that which is of greater value to me.

Ancient stories tell of persons giving away all that they own for some noble, if obscure, purpose. These stories have been told throughout history in every part of the world. In some of the tales, the purpose seems unclear even to the person making the sacrifice. The theme of these varied tales seems to be a kind of second beginning, a new birth in life.

Simple religious zealots, forever in trouble because they substitute passion for unhurried understanding, often misinterpret moral tales. They may rush to give away earthly belongings in the hope that they will receive eternal life in Paradise. It is a simple, greedy attempt to win a contest or strike a profitable bargain.

Having failed to learn the lessons inherent in the states of Necessary Contradiction and Commitment, they do not understand the folly of such childish greed.

Some people eat little meat, poultry, or fish because they can't afford them. Some stop eating them because they hope to improve health or lengthen life. Others "give up meat for Lent," or in some other way attempt to prove that they are able to control appetite and lust. But some people stop eating such food because they prefer not to take the lives of other creatures. Such people enjoy a gain, rather than suffer loss. The "sacrifice" is an appreciation of life, allowing them to shed the unwanted, unnecessary and undesired.

Emma was fifty-six years old when Arnold, thirty-one years old at the time, brought news that changed her forever. They had lived across the hall from one another for three years. Emma was a bookbinder who worked at home, and Arnold was a freelance photographer and public relations specialist who also worked out of his apartment. Emma had been living there for two years when Arnold moved in. Like people who spend much time alone, Emma was curious about any changes in her environment so she invited Arnold in for a glass of wine.

"I knew I liked him right away," she told me. "He had such a great sense of humor, and we both have the gift of gab. We got right down to the essentials. He was not in a relationship, but was dating. I was in one that I was out of every other month. Our pretty screens lasted less than a minute, and then we knew his ex was named Harvey and my sometimes-current was named Rosemary. The rest was easy. We used to slide notes under each other's door. Once he left one saying, 'Bind those pages, press that prose. I found you a girl, and her name is *Rose*.' Rose turned out to be nice but not that nice."

Arnold saw Emma through a year of gray days after she and Rosemary had decided to stop torturing one another and Rosemary moved to Cleveland. Then Arnold took Emma, as his date, to a very chic and proper party where she met Julie, the wife of a publisher Arnold wanted to impress. "I hate to sound so banal, but it was really love at first sight. And good old Otto had plans to run off with his secretary anyway, so it was like one of those Hollywood movies from the forties. Except Arnold was still bouncing around, dating, going to the baths and pretending to be cheerful about his loneliness."

Arnold, Julie, and Emma became a threesome on social occasions. "Let's face it," Emma said. "As I told him, he might be stuck with two dykes as dates, but it sure made him look like a ladies' man in that public relations world — as if any of us worried about such things. The three of us had a lot of good times. We could turn the dullest event into fun just by being together."

A year after Emma met Julie, Steven appeared. "Actually, he didn't appear so much as barge in," Emma said. "We were at some event or other and bored to tears. So we huddled in the corner and Steven just walked right over and pulled up a chair. Julie and I both liked him instantly. What was not to like? He is gorgeous, smart, educated, rich and a sweet guy besides. And he clearly had his eye on Arnold. It was the first time Julie and I ever excused ourselves so quickly. We looked over our shoulders and there was no doubt about it, we were not missed."

A few months later Arnold and Steven had bought a house together. Emma and Julie were still living separately because Julie wanted to wait until she was certain that her two girls would not be unsettled living with two lesbian mothers.

"Then, bang!" Emma said. "It was off as quickly as it was on. Steven had been determined to have a monogamous relationship and Arnold couldn't bring himself to make the promise. It scared him too much to think of being sexually tied to only one person after he had spent so many years passing for straight. He hadn't sowed his wild oats yet. But who could know what was coming?"

Two months after Steven and Arnold separated, Arnold was able to get his old apartment back, across the hall from Emma. "A month after that was the day he came and told me. His face was like a mask. 'The doctor did a biopsy. It's positive. I've got KS.' We just fell into one another's arms and cried and cried. There was nothing to say."

It was one of the early cases of AIDS. "Steven came back, offering friendship and money. They definitely weren't lovers anymore, but we marveled at how much closer they became as time went by. Both of them said it was beyond what either of them had hoped for in a lover relationship."

Julie took a backseat, supportive and willing to yield the time and energy Emma needed to devote to Arnold. Steven later told me, "It was a revelation for all of us. I have never seen anyone change so much in thirteen months as the four of us did, particularly Emma, Arnold and me. But it was new for Julie too, to be willing to wait, away from stage center, because it was the best she could contribute."

I took a drive into the country with Emma a few days after Arnold's memorial service. "I feel like I want to sleep all day for a month, and I miss Steven and Julie," she explained. "But something tells me to get off into the woods. I know you'll let me babble or be quiet." Intimate fragments of the story continued to surface throughout the day.

"You know, until these last thirteen months, I don't think I knew what love was," Emma said. "Oh, I thought I knew. And then when Arnold started to get sick I thought, 'Okay, this is where I make my commitment and give it all I have and hope it's enough.' You know, Steven or I were with him every minute that he wanted someone. He died in our arms."

She told me the same thing Steven said weeks later. "I never knew what love was. The three of us taught each other love in thirteen months. It wasn't an act of will. I didn't just *decide* to take care of Arnold. We took care of one another and the love got deeper and deeper. We told the truth as I have never heard it told. The three of us would cuddle on the bed together because we felt so lonely apart."

In Emma's words, "It wasn't willpower. I just gave in to it more and more. I let myself go and did what I *needed* to do. I needed to hold Arnold when he was dying. He needed it too. But I wasn't doing it because it was a decision to do something that would help Arnold. I did it because I had let go and could feel myself opening up more and more. I had no choice. I was down to bare bones. There was nothing else. It was simple. I found myself in a way I never knew I would. It still makes me cry. The love that Julie and I have is so much deeper now. Those special times when we're so close that we're one, Julie sometimes says, 'Thank you, Arnold.' And I blubber."

She had learned the lesson of the state of Sacrifice. Commitment can seem to be responsibility to be shouldered, and sometimes it is. But there is a further commitment that is simplification beyond one's will. It is possible to put on the brakes, to stop yourself from experiencing it. But if you do go ahead — give up, give in, let go and let yourself be as you are — you find what you must do. There was no choice about the commitment to the baby seal on the beach. And there was no choice about the letting go of all else, in sacrifice for gain, with Arnold.

Sacrifice yields more, not less. It is not martyrdom. It is a happy charity in which one sheds the unnecessary baggage accumulated in life. It is the state in which one discovers how self must move through pain and joy. It is the state in which one learns the wrong of selfishness, pretension, arrogance, greed, carelessness and all human attitudes that impede that simple, natural, forward movement of the self.

BALANCE

Conception is the state of conscious awareness in which new understanding is created from the union of old. It is a place of beginnings. Darkness and Blinding Light are the two states of conscious awareness in which society acts to forge the individual who, in turn, flees from growing imprisonment towards a truth and freedom that are too simple to be durable. In the state of Necessary Contradiction, the apparent opposites in the same person or same human action are seen, accepted and integrated. Strength is developed. Assumptions are questioned, personal values examined, and the true self glimpsed. In the linked states of Commitment and Sacrifice, one sheds the wraps of personal importance that have obscured natural form. Integrity demands a willing assumption of responsibility before revealing that satisfaction in life is to be found only when you are your own unique self.

In the state of Balance one finds peace. Constant turbulent changes continue as one revisits the states of Conception, Darkness, Blinding Light, Necessary Contradiction, Commitment and Sacrifice, but a graceful agility develops with the flexibility of acceptance. Balance is in the nature of constant changing motion.

I was a twenty-year-old college student when I met Grace. She was the director of the progressive elementary school where I finished my work-study program for college. My first glimpse of her was seeing her take out the garbage. She laughed and said, "Well, everyone has to take out the garbage sometime, I think, don't you?"

She had an endless curiosity about the world and its people, young and old. She was interested in every aspect of nature. She wanted the illiterate to discover the world of words and she wanted the literate to discover how to create with hands and heart. She wanted everyone to learn the worth of work and the joy of puttering.

She baked wonderful, wholesome bread, told stories about her varied experiences, read poetry by her fireplace, took long walks in the woods, watched birds, and listened.

Through the many years I knew her, I would find myself talking to her about my problems in person or in my mind. She had a unique ability to "worry" about the problem with you as she listened. She would admit that there seemed to be no solution. Having given up the hope of an answer, I would then list alternatives, usually concluding by saying what I thought I had to do. Then she would look grave, nod her head, and say, "If that's what you have to do, then you must do it." She was a natural healer and caretaker.

We were taking a walk through the woods near her house one cold winter day and I could feel her thoughtful preoccupation. The school was having a serious financial crisis. "Well," she said aloud in the middle of her thoughts, "I suppose the school may just have to close."

"That would be terrible, Grace," I said. "What would you do?"

She seemed startled and laughed. "Me? Oh, I guess I'll do the next thing." She bent down examining the earth. I thought she had found some treasure of a fungus or a rare winter flower.

"What do you see?" I asked, stooping next to her.

"I was noticing how the new things keep growing out of the old," she said. "You know, if the school closes, something new will grow out of it. Look at this rich, dark earth that grows from decay. It must take a hundred years to make an inch of top soil."

I did not know it then, but I now know that Grace lived in the state of Balance much of the time. When she died at ninety-four, I remembered a conversation I had with her when she retired in her seventies "so that new people can do new things." She said, "Now I can pay attention to death and things like that. Think of how little we know about it! It must be the grandest adventure of life." It is difficult to miss her because she is so much with me, and I know she is free at last to be off on her grand adventure.

Movement through the states of conscious awareness is a process. It does not follow a straight line, it follows your developmental needs. I think of Grace sitting in her rocking chair, near the warmth and light of the flames in her big fireplace. It was snowing outside and she was reading some of Whitman's poetry to me and my friend. Her favorite was *There Was Child Went Forth*. Everything that the child saw and experienced became a part of that child. She had put the book down in her lap when she finished reading and we thought she had dozed off. But she raised her head, the light of the flames shining on her moist eyes. "Isn't it nice when happiness sneaks up behind you and hugs you?" she asked. "I was thinking about how things keep changing and changing, yet how wonderful and happy it is with the three of us here, right now."

Balance.

Spirituality

We gay people are now able to speak openly about spiritual development. Just as we learned there was no need to be ashamed of our sexuality, we learned there is no need to be ashamed of our spirituality. A part of our desire to live is our desire to be healthy. We have learned to do what we can to develop our health. We know that healthy growth and development require the nourishing of body, intellect, emotions and spirit. We have learned that our spirit is not always well nourished by religious institutions. We are learning to find our own ways now.

Loneliness has been a problem for many of us. The loss of friends and lovers in the AIDS epidemic has stirred that old loneliness. We know we will get on with life. But for many of us there is a feeling of "I've been here before."

People who feel different early in life know a loneliness that is more profound than the experience of being temporarily separated from those with whom one shares emotional ties. Though we may learn to be adept at social interaction, loneliness unseen by others can be a constant companion.

I have witnessed the emergence of this fact countless times in the process of psychotherapy. At first I mistook it for the basic human loneliness that many psychotherapists presume to be the result of separating from the mother during the birth process. But the loneliness of the person who feels different is more stark.

A man who had been trapped alone during a mining accident described his hours of waiting and wondering if he would be found as similar to the early years of his life. "I was in no great physical pain and there was plenty of time to think and re-member," he said. He described the dim light that filtered into the chamber where he was imprisoned.

"I sat there and watched dust moats circulate in the light," he said. It reminded him of having sat alone, watching dust moats move in the slanting rays of afternoon sun when he was a young-ster. "I remembered watching them circulate, each speck like a star in a universe that never stops moving. It made me wonder if the end was going to be like the beginning and then I realized it's always been the same, through almost all the years. People around or no people around, I've usually been kind of lonely. There's been something missing no matter who I was involved with."

It was said differently by a very young woman who had gone through great troubles leaving her home in Central America. "For those years, all I could think of was getting to someplace where I could get work and feel safe. Those were real problems. They had priority. But even then, when I had a spare minute, I felt that loneliness come back. I have to admit I didn't feel that I belonged anywhere."

If the person feels different at an early age because of some difference of emotional, physiological or anatomical makeup that is known to family and neighbors, there is some hope of compas-sion. Others can be cruel about such differences, but they are often able to transcend their limitations, especially if the person is close to them.

The young person whose difference is not visible, however, seldom receives the needed reassurance from family, friends and community. A man who grew up on a farm said that family and friends had been very helpful to his older sister, who had lost the full use of one leg because of polio at age eight. "We had all kinds of special arrangements so she wouldn't feel too different. I guess it helped. They didn't know about me, of course. Being gay didn't show. When I came back from Korea without my left hand they tried to be good about it, but it was hard for them and it was hard for me. But when they found out I was gay, there was no attempt at understanding. I had to leave. It was too hard for me and my family."

Young people whose difference is not visible or known to family and neighbors often manage to spend a lot of time alone. This time spent alone, although compounding the loneliness, can have its value; it permits the youngster to invent ways of finding comfort in distraction. At the very least, the time alone permits a temporary opportunity to relax social viligance and enjoy some increased sense of safety, as well as a chance to indulge in nonconforming reflection.

I have heard stories of huts built in the woods, "secret hideaways" in attics, country treetops and city rooftops, caves, and long walks where "other people didn't go." Time spent alone in nature is often remembered as a time of relief — feeling not different, or whole, or acceptable. Though I have heard these stories many times, it is difficult to hear the familiar theme without feeling sad for the lonely child who learns to go away from the human community to find some sense of security and acceptable individuality.

Youngsters who spend time alone voluntarily have the chance to exercise imagination, fantasy, patience, a quiet sense of acceptance, and a subtle sense of appreciation. They often become reflective. Sometimes they become avid readers or musicians. Almost always, they use the experience of voluntary time away from other people to build inner resources. As adults they are less likely to be bored. This picture is changing today for children who are able to escape by entering the world of television. For these children there is the danger of becoming dependent on a source of distraction not of their own making. The form of their fantasy life may be programmed by strangers so unlike them that internal emotional conflict is intensified. And the situation is complicated by television's apparent philosophy that conflict is best resolved by violent action.

For the young person who seeks solitude and is not emotionally kidnapped by television, the time alone is lonely, but offers respite from conflict and fear. It also offers the invaluable experience of being accepted in a state of nature. For such youngsters, it is the beginning of spiritual awareness. Most gay people can remember these early times of life.

A man who is a poet today told me, "I didn't know how to name it then, and even today the right words are hard to find. There were moments of tranquility when I had my place in the infinite and all the rest faded to foolish background clutter."

A lesbian who was the caretaker of six younger siblings told me, "When the next oldest could take over, sometimes I'd go up the fire escape and sit on the roof. I could see the river and feel the sun or the rain and wind. I'd pretend I had a magic boat that went from the roof to the river and carried me to mountains far away. Everything was okay then. I imagined flowers and birds I'd never seen. And I'd find myself talking out loud — as if all that imagined place knew me and understood my thoughts. It made me feel that I was more than okay."

Such lonely young people often develop an intense, though perhaps poorly articulated, search for spiritual understanding. Big questions are considered. "Who am I?" "Who are they?" "How should we be with one another?" "Why am I alive?"

It is not unusual for such a young person to be drawn to nature, to religion, or to community groups in the search for the answers. As one man said, "I was a busy kid, checking out every church I could find, and all the clubs that would let me get a foot in the door. The other guys were there because they thought they had to be or should be. I was there because I thought I was missing something, and I was. But I never found what was missing in those places. I found it sometimes when I was out on the lake alone in a canoe. See, I missed that feeling of belonging. I belonged on the lake but not in church. It seemed weird."

In nature we learn to accept what we experience and do not understand. What is in nature simply is. And the changes that happen there simply happen. None of it requires explanation, no matter how odd it is. Such experiences in nature are compatible with the gay youngster's growing awareness of her own "difference." It makes it easier to accept the inner truth of our spiritual search without having to find reasons for it.

There is a natural bonding of spirituality and integrity. They grow together. It is quite common for the gay youngster to be devoted to organized religion. But, since most organized religions insist on conformity, and do not recognize the goodness of homoeroticism, that young person is unable to maintain both integrity and devotion. Some stay and attempt intricate systems of internal compromise and rationalization. Many, in order to continue the development of spirituality and integrity, are forced to leave.

In some times, places and cultures we have been respected as spiritual leaders, seers and healers, but it is hard to find such havens today. We continue to account for a large percentage of ministers and priests but are seldom able to be openly gay in these settings. Religious organizations continue to depend upon us and be threatened by us.

We are often banned, and have sometimes been burned, as witches or heretic "faggots." Conformists who need and cannot grasp our spirituality are driven by their ignorance and fear to try to destroy us. We represent the unknown, that which is beyond ordinary understanding, contained as it is by conformity.

An internationally acclaimed musicologist whose expertise is sacred music spent many years as a church organist and choir director. He said, "If they could ever be successful in getting us out of the churches, they would have no music." A priest who overheard him said, "They'd have no churches, so they wouldn't need the music."

As the social revolution ignited by World War II gathered momentum in the 1970s, it became more and more clear that lesbians and gay men are not a small minority of the population. Gay people who were still involved in organized religion experienced a crisis of conscience. They pressured the institutions to acknowledge gay people as respected members. That political struggle for honesty continues.

The arrival of the AIDS epidemic in the international gay community accelerated our spiritual development in a way previously unmatched. We would do what we could to help traditional religious organizations, but it was imperative that we tend our own spiritual maturation in every way possible. After a decade in which we celebrated the right and responsibility to live as the people we are — a decade in which we faced the questions posed by meeting life honestly — we now faced the questions suddenly posed by meeting death honestly.

Four years ago I talked with a young man who had spent much of his life seeking answers to spiritual questions. He put it plainly. "Two years ago I was running as fast as I could, literally and figuratively. I had discovered that I was a jock as well as a theological bookworm. I had also discovered that I was sexually attractive to a lot of other men. I was very busy learning how to live and how to love. Now I'm moving more slowly, with the help of this cane, and still learning how to live and how to love. But now I have to learn how to die as well. It's a lot to learn in a few years."

The advent of the AIDS epidemic helped us to move more rapidly into Commitment and Sacrifice as states of conscious awareness. We already had more than a little experience with the state of Necessary Contradiction. We had lived our lives knowing that our natural loving, caring, and erotic feelings were in contradiction to the orientation prescribed by our society. And we learned that our spiritual growth contradicted the limited avenues of expression permitted by the religious establishment. In the cauldron of these basic contradictions, the strength of our integrity was formed. It was, therefore, not as surprising as it seemed that we reacted to the AIDS crisis so quickly with our commitment. Our already-formed integrity demanded it.

While each of us, as individuals, were following our own developmental path of awareness as a gay person, collectively our integrity had been formed. We were ready to act with commitment. Sacrifice helped us more quickly shed the burden of ennui that had begun to accumulate when we discovered we were more than the primarily sexual beings we had been trained to believe we were. Having moved rapidly into the conscious awareness found in the states of Commitment and Sacrifice, we discovered the state of Balance and caught a glimpse of the whole of conscious awareness.

That glimpse at the whole of human conscious awareness has been a powerful, awesome reminder of the spiritual nature of lesbians and gay men. We are more than people who can enjoy homosexuality. Many non-gay people have discovered pleasures to be found in same-gender sexual intercourse. We gay men and lesbians are different. We have a different orientation than the average person. By nature and training, we see from what is considered both the male and the female point of view in a society. We have the potential for a balanced view and a balanced understanding.

In glimpsing the whole of conscious awareness, we became aware that we have the capacity to develop a balanced view and a balanced understanding far beyond that which is comfortable for the conformity-oriented person. We can more easily begin to understand the interrelatedness of present, past and future as a balanced whole. We can more easily accept the workings of the universe and the small vital place we humans occupy in it. It is a potential responsibility available to people who have been forced to develop their conscious awareness. Not all such people are gay and not all gay people can shoulder this responsibility, so wonderful that one has no choice but to be extremely humbled by it.

It must be true that people have traveled to this point of spiritual awakening in every generation. The remarkable phenomenon now presenting itself to the world is a large segment of the population reaching this point of spiritual awareness together, at the same time. We have traveled a spiritual path in two decades that could easily take a lifetime. The wisdom of old age is combined with the vigor of youth. Whatever grows from the seed of this beginning, the understanding we gay people have of ourselves will never be the same. We are finding that which was missing, the conscious recognition of our spirituality. From this small beginning it seems likely that the human world will be changed in some way.

I know a nurse who was once a nun. When the AIDS epidemic arose, she was one of many who volunteered to work on an AIDS ward before any of us knew whether it was safe to do so. "My family always used to say there were no atheists in foxholes," she said. "I don't know about that. I just think a foxhole must be a terrifically bad place for a very spiritual person to be. You'd have to be asking yourself what business you have being involved in killing. Some of the most spiritual people I know are atheists, or have been for some chunk of their lives. I can't imagine a God who'd get all huffy and insulted if you ignored His existence. That sounds more like a Mother Superior than a God. But I sure can imagine a God who would accept the painful fact that people get hurt when they fight against their own nature. You have to let life happen if you have any faith at all."

We met because I was at the hospital to see a man who was dying. He had grown up in a staunchly religious home but had left the church when it insisted that being gay made him a bad person. On one of my visits he said, "I've got great news. God and I are on speaking terms again. We're chatting every day. I guess it's prayer. I'd lost track of it somewhere along the line when they were giving me religious instruction, but we're back on the line now and it's great."

I asked if he had told his family. "Oh, hell no," he said. "They'd think I was crazy. This is like it was when I was a kid. I used to sit in the tree fort and look at the sky and think things over. But now I remember it was more like talking things over with someone, or something, or whatever. That was real prayer and I'm into it again, thank God."

With the advent of AIDS we saw that we would have to do everything we could to push governmental and medical establishments to provide adequate care and to seek the means of prevention and cure. We knew it would not be easy, because AIDS was seen by the ruling establishments as a disease affecting only an unrespected minority group. We knew that in the meantime we would have to give from our private resources in the gay community and gratefully accept the help of our non-gay friends. We did not realize at first that AIDS would expose the established spiritual leaders to a test that most would fail in full public view. Clever rationalizations and thinly disguised personal prejudice wear thin with the public when good people are dying.

Many so-called spiritual leaders frantically protected their vested interests and showed themselves to be merely chief executive officers and stockholders. At the same time, we gays became more clearly spiritual in orientation and showed ourselves to be capable of responsible, loving behavior. We would do what we must to promote human life and worth, while accepting what must be accepted.

We have had our sick to care for, our dying to comfort and be comforted by, and our dead to mourn. We have been forced to accept the gift of each day and to live it as best we can, with appreciation.

The man who rediscovered his childhood penchant for prayer while in the hospital told me that many of his friends were doing the same. Shortly before he died he said, "Funny, isn't it? We're the ones with faith. I've begun to see how it all fits together. Dying will be fine. The God I trust is the whole shebang — everything — way beyond this little solar system. Certainly not a He or a She. But I can say 'God.' It's as good a name as anything. How could I not trust this God? It would be silly. But my brothers and sisters are still on their knees trying to make business deals with some guy in a dress sitting on a cloud. They don't have much faith."

A gay priest who had become his friend was with him when he died. "Boy, I sure hope I get where he was before I die," he told me. "He taught me a lot. For him, God was life, love and change. I've been studying this almost all my life and he just knew it. The day before he passed away he told me not to forget about life, love and change. Then he winked at me and said, 'A few good laughs and some great sex are included at no extra charge.'"

As we find our spirituality, nourish it, and share it with one another, we are less lonely. We are finding what was missing.

Cooperating with Change

As change continues to enter our lives, we have a choice. We can fight it, becoming exhausted in the struggle, or we can embrace it, moving with it in the best possible harmony. The choice is not between aggression and submission. The choice is between a struggle or a cooperative dance. Cooperation is co-operation. We cannot control change in this life and it need not control us. We can learn to maintain a graceful balance as we meet and move with change, even though the change often takes us by surprise.

It was a sunny Sunday morning and I was enjoying my orange juice when the phone rang. It was my friend Gary and his tone was not as light as usual. His doctor had given him the diagnosis of KS the day before. It was early in the epidemic, and he was the first of my friends to be diagnosed. The clarity of that moment is vividly preserved.

What could I do? What could he do? Both of us knew little about the disease, except that it threatened his life and there was no known treatment. He confessed that he was afraid. He had decided to leave his job in one week and devote himself to learning all that he could about the disease and how to fight it. He had disability insurance and medical insurance that would take care of his financial needs. Now he needed the emotional support of his friends and he needed to learn.

We talked to talk, to reassure one another that we were in communication. We both knew that it was best to focus on fighting the disease and learning more about it. The enormous change that had entered his life could not be fought. His responding changes would have to help him stay balanced.

Sweet, easy-going, searching Gary was finding his footing that morning, seeking balance. He was afraid, but wise enough to know that he must embrace the unexpected change. His fight would be with the disease, not with the change that had come and those that would follow.

Humans, capable of conscious thought and reflection, are easily disabled by fear. We fear the unknown and often permit that fear to paralyze us. We fail to show love, for fear of rejection. We fail to try, for fear of failure.

When not frozen by our fear of the unknown, we are tempted to go to the opposite extreme of trying to predict and control the future. Our fear does us more harm than the unforeseen change. Our struggles to control the future for ourselves are as unsuccessful as our attempts to control the weather. Worry, fear, and the illusion of control do not help. Trust in one's developed ability to cooperate with change does help. We cannot control the future but we can learn to change ourselves and move forward in harmony.

Two years ago, an exhausted woman came to my office for consultation. After several years of denial, she had admitted that her lover was addicted to drugs. Her attempt to control her lover and the substance abuse had led to her own lack of emotional balance. It took months for her to see that she could only change herself and that the active addiction was her lover's problem.

Fear had caused the denial and the exhausting attempts to fix that which she could not fix. She was afraid of changes that might enter her life because of her lover's addiction. She feared the loss of love, and she feared social disgrace. Her heroic attempts to block the forces of change had been costly to her, and to her lover. It was more than a year before she began to trust herself, and life, again. Only then could she entertain the possibility that she might cooperate with changes the future would bring.

We gay people have experienced more than our fair share of confusion about love, caring and sex. When we were young, the love and care given us was on the condition that we not reveal our true feelings. It was clear to us that, if we unmasked the true self, the love and care would be revoked. This wreaked havoc with any true sense of security and with developing self-esteem. But it did help us develop resilience so that we were ready to cope with whatever might come our way. Most gay people know very well that the future is unpredictable. We know that sudden change can come with little or no warning. We learned early in life to live with the threat of exposure and its unpredictable consequences.

Many of us fell into the trap for some period of time of trying to control the future by fixing the unfixable. It is a tempting illusion. It looks as if security and peace might wait at the end of that road. But we have learned already to expect the unexpected, and are not destroyed when we find the road dead ends in exhaustion and defeat. We turn back, ready to embrace change, ready to continue the dance.

It takes us time to learn to trust the love and care offered to us, and it takes time to learn to trust the love and care we offer others. Having grown up surrounded by conditional love, which sought to control us by suppressing our true identity, we are wary of illusion and the bruises it inflicts. We must learn to get past the temptation to control with offers of love. Satisfaction resides, ultimately, in giving and receiving the real thing with no strings attached.

Sex as an expression of love and care can also be quite confusing. As youngsters, we were taught that our erotic orientation to some people of the same gender was wrong. Our erotic orientation led us to feel loving, protective, and sexual toward people who, we were told, should be our rivals. It was a confusing and perplexing experience.

Bolstered by the contemporary re-examination of social mores and values, we fought to put our lives right again. We knew intuitively that our attractions were loving and caring. We had to struggle with the lies that surrounded us and the prejudice we had internalized while growing up. We learned that our sexual attraction to one another was not wrong, even if the sudden change that came with the permissive social revolution had us off balance sometimes.

We reached out to one another sexually in our determination to gain our footing and find our truth. And the increased permission to become more vulnerable with one another in sexual sharing did help us to bond more strongly as a group. The sexual friendliness reminded us that we could easily love and care for one another.

But unexpected change waited in the wings. The physical vulnerability that is a part of genuine sexual intimacy made us vulnerable to a new and deadly viral disease. By the time it became visible in the gay male community, the catastrophe was well under way.

Momentous change entered our lives. We had no choice but to embrace this change and find our footing once again. While we were able to respond quickly with the commitment and sacrifice needed to provide one another with care, our loving naturally became confused once again. We had barely gained our freedom to begin the exploration of intimacy and sexuality. We had not had many years to make the mistakes that are natural while learning to trust one another and be vulnerable. This disease made it tempting to distrust one another sexually and, hence, to distrust vulnerability and intimacy. Yet we had to find our ways to cooperate with this change.

Within a few years, although distracted by our fears, sickness and mourning, we found ways to cooperate with this change. We developed the concept of safe sex — sexual practices based on constantly updated medical information that would make it most unlikely for the virus to be passed from one person to another. Safe-sex practices led us to focus more clearly on how we expressed our love and care in these careful sexual practices. Sexually exclusive monogamy quickly gained in popularity also.

During our years of exploration and discovery we had learned to touch one another more freely, literally and figuratively. As we continue to find our cooperative response to the changes the disease brought into our lives, we gay men find we need that bodily affection we had begun to take for granted. Massage has gained rapidly in popularity. And we are trying to find cooperative ways of fighting the sexual confusion and regaining the good of our collective sexual bonding. Telephone sex and masturbation clubs were innovative steps in that direction. Our new ways continue to emerge.

We know that the enemy to be fought is not our bonding, intimacy, vulnerability or sexuality. That becomes increasingly clear as we become increasingly free of the confusion stirred by the change. The enemy to be fought is the disease. We must fight the disease, not the change it has brought. We must, as usual, embrace the unexpected change and find our way to cooperatively turn it to advantage. We know that we can and must find ways to be more satisfyingly intimate, sexual and vulnerable in our loving and caring for one another. We have learned to trust our ability to cooperate with change.

We have learned that our greatest strength grows from our support of one another. Just as we learned the great value of physical contact, we learned the value of emotional support during times of change. When we were lonely, isolated individuals, we felt weak. When we began to find one another in our marvelous variety and great number, we felt our strength. Our strength is in a community that is strikingly diverse, a community of gay men and lesbians ready and willing to offer support to one another.

We have learned not only to cooperate with the changes that enter our lives unexpectedly, but also to work persistently for desired change. If we did not continue to do so, our civil rights would be once more in danger. We cooperate. We accept the reality of the status quo and seek to change it in a peaceful, nonviolent manner.

Neither a rigid social order nor revolution provide safety for gay people. Revolution is too risky for people who have suffered the consequences of confusion and conformity. Our safety resides in social *evolution*. Revolution turns things upside down and causes great confusion. When the dust settles, successful revolutionaries are apt to become tomorrow's rigid rulers. We gay men and lesbians have no guarantee that any rigid social order will favor our diverse nonconforming minority.

The evolving course of social change favors lesbians and gay men. Although there are flare-ups of bigotry and prejudice, the world is slowly moving toward appreciation of diversity. Elected representatives from minority groups are more common now; for some, their minority status has been an asset.

A non-gay man told me that he had voted for a gay person for public office "because I think I can trust a person who has the guts to be truthful and run against prejudice. Maybe we won't always agree, but it will be honest disagreement. There won't be a bunch of hidden agendas."

Lesbians and gay men have shown remarkable courage in working for social change. We have demonstrated our ability to adapt to the current reality while persistently working for changes we believe to be justified. In so doing, we have become a vital part of the new, evolving, nonviolent social morality.

Not very long ago in human history, might made right. Morality was a contest, and the winner was "right" because the battle had been won. Too often the defeated were "wrong" because they had less money or fewer weapons. We are just beginning to find our way to a morality based on nonviolent demonstrations of conscience.

I recently talked to a young man who is an exemplary representative of the emerging nonviolent morality based on freshly examined individual conscience. He is a non-gay college student, and he has a gay friend named Fred who was his roommate during freshman year. "So Fred and his lover had this idea of starting a little demonstration every day in front of the Administration Building to protest discrimination against gay faculty spouses not getting the same health benefits as faculty wives or husbands."

It was to be a modest protest. Fred and his lover planned to meet each weekday at noon when there were the most people out on campus. They would put their books down, embrace and kiss one another for a full minute.

"You should have seen the crowd they drew the first day. The second day they got jumped by some guys from a fraternity. So the third day my friend Joe, who's also straight, and I decided to join them. It was kind of risky and kind of fun. When Joe and I kissed, these frat guys really freaked out. I thought we were going to get jumped too, but then our girlfriends stood up alongside us and they kissed each other. Well, frat guys can't hit girls in public. Pretty soon there were all kinds of people kissing each other and laughing together. It was great!"

An older lesbian was quite articulate in explaining her place in the evolving nonviolent morality. "I was a Lieutenant Colonel in the army, and quite comfortable in giving orders. Later I got lots of splinters climbing the corporate ladder. Then I was a heavy-duty spokesperson in the women's movement, which led straight into an important political appointment where I was supposed to be window dressing and follow orders. One day I asked myself what business I had giving or taking orders. I know what I think is right today, but it may be different tomorrow. The "right" thing for me to do is search my conscience every day and stay in integrity with myself throughout the day. With enough of us doing that, the right changes will come, even if I don't like all of them. I'm not God. I don't know if *my* right is the *most* right. "

The most visible representatives of the evolving nonviolent morality are sometimes the victims of the violence they have transcended. Yet the killing of such respected world figures as Gandhi and Martin Luther King, Jr. has strengthened the resolve of millions of people, enabling them to overcome their own fears and join the ranks of the nonviolent moralists.

Lesbians and gay men are familiar with the ways in which our own fears can imprison us. Each of us has had to struggle with the conflict about whether to continue to hide the true self or to "come out" by disclosing our gay identity. We know the damage to self-esteem that can be done by our secrets and our fears. We must learn to trust the evolving world and to trust our own ability to cooperate with change if we hope to overcome the fears that imprison us.

An older gay man told me, "The first time a friend of mine was diagnosed with AIDS, I was so scared I got right down on my knees and started scrubbing the kitchen floor. My grandma used to say that not everybody knows how to pray, but everybody knows how to get on their knees. She said while you're there you may as well scrub the kitchen floor because it probably needs doing anyway, and it's a good reminder that you can make some things better while you're figuring out if you can let God make the other things better." That seemed to me a good way to practice humility and trust while remembering how to cooperate in the course of change. We cannot control the future and we cannot control the weather but that man's grandmother probably would agree that we can be willing to change and be smart enough to get out of the rain when a bad storm comes.

Near the end of his life Gary told me that he was no longer afraid. "I used to be afraid of anger, but it's only anger," he said. "And I guess I was afraid of dying, but it's only the next change."

He told me about going to the park when he had the energy. He regularly met two women there. One fed the seagulls and the other the pigeons. They were good-natured, protective competitors.

"We were worried one morning when the pigeon lady was late," he said. "Her birds finally heard her old car coming and they flew around, all excited. She was late because she was tending a bird with a broken wing that she had taken home."

Gary noticed a number tattooed to her arm. "She said she came to the birds each day because she remembered that when she was in the camp there were no birds, but she said the birds started coming back when the shooting stopped. She said they reminded her every day to go toward peace. 'They trust me and I trust them, even if I can't get them to do what I want and they can't get me to do what they want. We get along.'"

Gary became a nonviolent, unafraid activist before he died, trying to persuade his government to provide funds to fight the disease. He did what he could. Good person that he was, he did his part to cooperate with change. He lived well.

Living in Time

A friend of mine first told me about Jon. My friend was attending a conservatory of music in Massachusetts but had returned to San Francisco in 1978 for a visit. He was waiting for the traffic light to change at the corner of Castro and Eighteenth Streets when Jon walked up to him cheerfully, pointed to the instrument case in his hand, and said, "Would you be interested in playing in a gay band?" Jon had turned a corner in his own life. After studying and teaching music for most of his thirty years, he wanted to help gay men and lesbians make music together and present it to the world. His enthusiasm was irrepressible.

I saw him in action not long after that. He presented an intense appreciation of life and music that was irresistible. He led a smart-stepping "Gay Freedom Day Marching Band and Twirling Corps" and a chorus; they were the first in a series of varied musical groups he was to organize and inspire during the next two years.

We were swept along by Jon's intensity, the brassy music and the sassy lyrics, as these men and women marched, played and sang out:

"If they could see me now
That little hometown clan
We're singing. and we're playing with this all-gay band
I'd like for all the world to see for a fact,
That we're a source of power they'll never send back.
The closet's empty now, just like it ought to be.
The time is right for us, just look around and see.
What a set up, holy cow,
They'd never believe it, If my friends could see me now."

It was a small sparkling army of joy that brought us to our feet, cheering, laughing and crying.

Those were intense years of new beginnings. Jon was helping to start all kinds of new musical groups, including a tap dancing troupe, a brass group, a woodwind quintet, and a classical music orchestra.

He and I met every half-dozen weeks for lunch. "Not for psychotherapy," as I said. "Just to get me combed out," as Jon said. He had endless hopes and dreams, and he got bruised at times in that peculiarly painful way that happens to private people who are public persons in their creative work. He was a man with a mission, still stunned by special moments — such as when the city's first elected gay supervisor, Harvey Milk, handed him an official city check to help support the struggling band. A day later, Milk was assassinated. "It's as if the baton passes to the next one," Jon said.

Jon died in July 1984. Months earlier, he had called me from his hospital room when he was diagnosed as having pneumonia. When I arrived at the hospital, his tiny isolation room was filled with flowers and people. It was before we knew that the disease was not transmitted by casual contact, so there was an ominous presence of masks, gloves and sterile gowns. More visitors waited in the hall. Jon asked if I would come back when we could talk alone. "Bring your comb," he said. "I need to get a few things clear." He was worried, as it turned out, that he might somehow have made himself more susceptible to the disease at times when he was discouraged or depressed. He wanted reassurance that he had not failed to appreciate the gift of life.

We didn't laugh as much in the hospital as we had at our lunches. But we did smile when Jon said, "Well, I guess I get to go over the rainbow after all," alluding to conversations in which we had mused on the fascination *The Wizard of Oz* holds for gay people, and the special meaning the lyrics "Somewhere over the rainbow" hold for us. After a short silence Jon said, "It seemed there was so much to do and so little time. Now there's all the time in the world."

We are taught a linear concept of "a lifetime," like a length of chain that has a beginning, a middle, and an end. The chain of lifetime we learn has one small link we call "now" connecting a past of determined length to a future of indeterminate length.

We think and speak of time in our lives in much the same way as we conceptualize money. We spend it, save it, manage it, waste it, use it wisely, hoard it, and squander it. We begin to believe that it is property, something belonging to us, for which we are responsible. The very rich and the very old are newsworthy.

People who are aware that death is near are sometimes able to escape from this concept of time. Once beyond its limitations, time can be experienced as never-ending change without form or shape. It is possible then to be aware of love without limiting it by segmenting past-love-lost and future-love-not-yet-found. Likewise, misery and pain can be accepted in entirety without our being drowned in its presence "now."

Acceptance of the nearness of death in life permits a greater perspective. It is possible to glimpse "this life" or "my life" as a part of all life, part of all change, two moments in the endless change being "this birth" and "this death." The identity we become accustomed to as "I" is product and participant in the endless change that is all life. The steel girder that seems so solid is no more and no less than a collection of molecules, each and all of which are constantly changing. There is no permanent form. Time is nothing more than change. Age, youth, joy and sadness are no more than places in that sea of change.

The morality that is evolving in conscious awareness during this century is less influenced by a linear concept of time and more influenced by an understanding of the dominant role of change in our experience of life. This evolving morality grows out of the traditional human values of loving and caring, but it is free of the preoccupation with time as a possession. It recognizes the futility of rigid conformity. While *life* is eternal, *my* life is temporary. This evolving morality places my attitudes and behavior in that perspective, one small *but vital* part of humanity as a whole. My responsibility is not the ownership and management of time, it is the harmonious placement of my life in the eternal flow of change.

Measured time is a quantitative concept that is the product of the human mind. The human mind has now become capable of a broader concept. We people who are different find ourselves in the vanguard of a new age of enlightenment. Gay people caught in the AIDS epidemic are being forced to look at how they measure value in human life. In a universe ruled by change rather than man-made time, the value of a life can be measured only by its quality, not its duration.

And that is why nonviolence is a central force in this evolving, more relevant morality. We humans are capable of rational reflection and choice. We have the responsibility to be honest with one another as we seek to improve the quality of life. We will disagree, but we dare not kill or even knowingly harm one another. To do so is to lessen the quality of all life and deny the value of all life. To harm another human being is to harm ourselves.

We have the responsibility to appreciate life and to increase the scope of conscious experience. As lesbians and gay men we have had to acknowledge our need to love and care for others of the same gender, even when our human communities forbade it. Many of us have tried to obey the rules of our communities and paid a price for it. When we try to conform to contemporary expectations we find that we are misusing life and denying our inner truth, and that by so doing we rob all life of its value rather than aiding in its appreciation. We have learned to be protective of our loving and caring. It is our responsibility.

I talked with a woman who moved her home two thousand miles to be with her son during the final months of his illness. A widow with no other children, she has decided to stay on for an indefinite period, sharing her mourning with his lover and his friends. "We became a close family in those final weeks," she told me. "I'm not in any shape to make the decision yet, but I am thinking about staying here and doing some volunteer work to help people with AIDS and their families."

In a not-unusual scenario, she did not know her son was gay until he wrote to tell her he had AIDS. He had chosen to put the thousands of miles between them rather than tell her about himself, because he feared she would not understand and he might lose her love.

"Since I've been here, I've heard a few stories of lovers who ran off in panic when the diagnosis was announced, and I wasn't shocked," she said. "Some people are weak, and you never know the whole story, anyway. What did surprise me was to meet Stevie's family here. I am so glad that he has had such good friends. And I feel lucky that they opened their arms and took me in, no questions asked."

She told of bedside vigils and emergency calls to friends at any hour of the night or day. "They taught me a lot about loving, living and dying," she said. "We always used the expression 'passed on' at home as a polite way to say somebody had died. But I began to see they meant it when they talked about passing on. I asked several of them where they thought a person passed on to and they said they didn't know — just 'on' — just changing and leaving the remains of a body and memories of having been."

One of his friends described to me how she had been holding her son's hand and watching him when he died. "It's true," she told me. "I was right there when he came into this world and I was right there when he left. It was his time. I don't know which was the greater blessing. Maybe it's all one. I miss being able to see him and touch him. But I still talk with him. I don't care if people think I'm crazy. I know he's passed on and I don't know where or what 'on' is. I know I'll pass on too. Until then I've got some things to do in this life."

A nurse who voluntarily works on a hospital ward where many AIDS patients die was asked how she could bear the constant partings. She said that it reminded her in some ways of working with newborns on a maternity ward. "It's more grown-up here," she said. "These people can tell me what hurts, and sometimes I can help. I can love and they can love. When the babies left the hospital I could imagine their future lives, but it was all my own projections. When these guys leave, it's hard to believe they're headed for anything bad. I've never been around people who were more appreciative. They've helped me appreciate my own life. I wouldn't trade my work with anybody. I think I'm living well."

There are many people who are so filled with fears that they hide from life, failing to appreciate it. Some are aware of their disability and some are not. Some who would recoil in horror at the thought of hitting, stabbing, or shooting another person are quite placid about sacrificing someone's life on the altar of their own fears.

When it became clear that the three usual modes of transmission of the AIDS virus were shared intravenous needles, sexual intercourse, and blood transfusion, a means was quickly found to screen donated blood to be sure it was safe. But fearful people living constricted lives found temporary relief in the thought that "those others" with AIDS were getting what they deserved.

As the gay community became increasingly successful with its safe-sex education programs, we realized that teenagers and the uneducated were the very high-risk groups for AIDS. But fear-ridden, pious people blocked efforts to talk about homosexuality, condoms, and needles in high schools. Though we know that sexual activity is high among poorly informed teenagers, fearful adults were quite willing to condemn many of them to death to avoid giving these young people "ideas" that might somehow encourage sexual experimentation — especially homosexual experimentation. The idea of making disposable needles available to drug addicts was equally unacceptable lest it lead such people to believe that their behavior was condoned. And so they too were sentenced to probable death.

To appreciate life, we must be able to accept it as it is. Before we can invest in life with enjoyment, love, care, and acceptance, we must achieve genuine humility before the majesty of all that we do not understand. I understand how this solar system works, in terms of the movements of planets orbiting our sun star that is also moving in the universe, but I do not understand what causes the beauty of a sunrise. I can only appreciate its magnificence.

Steve's mother was one of the first to volunteer to try to get into high schools to talk to teenagers. "I am sixty-two years old and not interested in sexually seducing any of those youngsters, male or female," she said. "I am also not interested in promoting promiscuity of any variety. But I'm not afraid to talk about death, life, sex, needles, or condoms, either. I might have been once, but I've done some growing up since I got here, and I hate to see some of these kids die before their parents can wake up and grow up. The price is too high. It's a terrible wrong to hoard life as if it were a savings account for the future. I believe I've learned we have to be willing to share the good and the bad — give life all we've got and take all it gives, and stop checking the balance."

Her sentiments were echoed when I told a gay 84-year-old Frenchman about her. "It's the worst to be stingy," he said. "All that I have now is from what I gave away. When I was younger and prettier I was generous. Some of the boys said I was being stupid but it has all come back with interest."

He said he thought we gay men and lesbians had to work at improving the generosity of our lovemaking and caring for one another "while there is still time." He told me we should appreciate that our lovemaking was not simply for propagation. "There's more than enough of that in the world," he said. "Even I did it when I was married. We gays have only to love and make more love. What I need and you have, you must give willingly. One has a good brain, one lots of money, old guys like me sometimes have wisdom, one has a heart everybody can trust, one makes his muscle big on those machines in the gym. Maybe one poor guy has nothing but being pretty, though usually not. But everybody has something to put in, and everybody needs. We had a little gang of gays in Europe like that after the First World War. If I care for you, I give you what I have, the best I can. It's not mine to keep anyway."

The ordeal of this decade seems to be teaching us these lessons. We are discovering what each of us has to offer that is of value to others in need. We are learning that we receive most in the giving. We are learning how better to care and be caretakers, how better to love and be lovemakers. The most difficult struggle, contrary to popular belief about gay people, has been to continue to value and improve the part that our sexuality plays in our caring and loving. As one man wryly said, "The old orgies were easy, this new sex is intense. Acrobatics isn't enough, you've got to put out from the soul. My roommate used to worry about whether someone would want to tie him up. Now he worries about whether someone will set him free." That seems to be true. We have tapped into our spirituality, and facades are no longer enough.

I liked the attitude a young lesbian displayed. She had been insulted by a woman who was a fellow worker in her office. "She started with put-downs about gay guys, then a bad joke about AIDS, and finally got around to how useless lesbians are because they don't build a God-fearing family like she's doing. Since she's pretty dumb, I decided not to take it personally. I just said I, for one, hadn't had any phone calls from God lately so I guessed this life was just a temporary assignment for me and I figured I'd better mind my own business and just do good where I could. I told her it looked like that would keep me plenty busy until the temporary assignment was wrapped up and it was time to pass on."

Certainly life on this planet is temporary, whether or not it is an assignment. To the extent that we can trust scientific predictions, all human life on this planet will end sooner or later — sooner if we are careless, later if we are careful. And each of us must be prepared to shed our identity, move along, and make way for those who are to follow. Perhaps it is the persistent reminders of the temporary nature of life that causes many people to fret about eternity, heaven, and hell. Superhuman and inhuman actions continue to be motivated by concerns about eternal comfort.

Limited as we all are by the abilities of the human mind and the experiences and learning possible in a lifetime, I can do little more as a person and a psychologist than to listen to such concerns with true compassion. Since time seems little more than a human concept designed to capture a glimpse of eternity, I am not shocked by the possibility of a subjective experience of heaven or hell for an eternity. One simple explanation might be the internal playback or unwinding of all thoughts, feelings, and experiences stored in one's brain as spirit leaves body and the system loses life. Was it not Omar Khayyam who "sent my soul into the invisible" to answer that concern, only to have it return with the message that "I, myself, am heaven and hell?" We do seem to create a heaven in our better moments and a hell in our worst times. So perhaps in less "time" than it takes the clock on the wall to tick from one second to the next, the brain's unwinding replay of a cumulative lifetime creates the subjective experience of eternity with one's very personal experience of heaven or hell. Such a possibility is additional motivation to do what one can to create heaven on earth within this lifetime.

We gay men and lesbians, people who are different, have no choice but to take ourselves as is, and life as we find it. We must accept, or suffer the consequences of self-deception. We must live our lives in time, whatever time there is, doing the best we can. We cannot please the conformists, and it would destroy their brittle civilization if we could.

The human world has need not only of women who are attracted to men and can love them, and men who are attracted to women and can love them; we also need women who are attracted to women and can love them, and men who are attracted to men and can love them. Homoerotic bonding is vital. Without the sane, if often invisible, balance of men who love men and women who love women — people who thrive in peace — the fighting and killing would quickly become truly insane and out of control.

It is difficult for some non-gay people to understand, yet every gay person has experienced it. Our attractions do not follow the rules of family, tribe or nation. We can and do catch one another's eye everywhere on the planet and there is instant recognition of our relatedness, though we may not speak a word to one another. Some of us have been pressed into presumably patriotic service in wartime. We can act as brave heroes and heroines, but killing, whether across national boundaries or across a backyard fence, is contrary to our general interests. We need one another and cannot be identified easily by skin color or national uniform.

Many people seek their roots, their homeland, the place that nurtured their ancestors. While there are places in the world that have been more appreciative and accepting of us at various times, our homeland is the entire planet. Our ancestors lived everywhere. We have been martyred in every way that people have been martyred. Yet we have quietly clung to our truth and found one another, around the world generation after generation. Our truth grew as we grew, and each of us found there came a time when we had to admit it to ourselves. With the admission comes the need to find one another anywhere in the world. This planet is sacred to us. So are its people, because it is from the people of the whole world that our future generations of gay people will come.

Two years before Jon's sickness appeared, he took time out and went traveling to other parts of the world. When he returned, we had fun talking about his experiences. "I grew and expanded in every possible way," he said, laughing, "just like the universe does. I even shifted my weight a little," he said patting his stomach. "Now I want to do some composing. I want to hear some music I've never heard." Later in our conversation he said, "Maybe the only sin most of us are guilty of is limiting ourselves."

We gay men and lesbians have grown older and wiser quickly in recent times. Our conscious awareness has brought us much closer to learning the ancient secret of cooperation with change. We are less limited. We are learning an agility of the human spirit that permits the peace of being balanced while in motion. We are loving, caring and changing, while experiencing the fullness of life and death.

There was a memorial service for Jon at San Francisco's magnificent Grace Cathedral in August 1984. It was for Jon, and it was for all of us who had gone before, and all who would follow.

There was a lot of love and a lot of care. And there was a lot of music. Appropriately, there were rainbows of balloons released from the high hill on which the cathedral stands. Up they went, freed from the planet, reaching, expanding, destined to continue beyond all rainbows — gay and changing.

A wide variety of books with gay and lesbian themes are available from Alyson Publications. For a catalog, or to be placed on our mailing list, please write to:
Alyson Publications
40 Plympton Street
Boston, Mass. 02118.